W9-BRE-426

	DATE DUE		
12-03-03 0			
JAN 0 3 2005			
JAN 1 8 2005			

BioCritiques

Bloom's BioCritiques

ERNEST HEMINGWAY

Edited and with an introduction by
Harold Bloom
Sterling Professor of the Humanities
Yale University

CHELSEA HOUSE PUBLISHERS
Philadelphia

©2002 by Chelsea House Publishers, a subsidiary of
Haights Cross Communications.

Introduction © 2002 by Harold Bloom.

Printed and bound in the United States of America

10 9 8 7 6 5 4 3 2 1

Library of Congress Cataloging-in-Publication Data

Ernest Hemingway / edited and with an introduction by Harold Bloom.
    p. cm. - (Bloom's bio critiques)
    Includes bibliographical references and index.
    ISBN 0-7910-6174-4
    1. Hemingway, Ernest, 1899-1961 —Criticism and interpretation. I. Bloom, Harold. II.
Series.

PS3515.E37 Z58655 2001
813'.52—dc21   2001053802

Chelsea House Publishers
1974 Sproul Road, Suite 400
Broomall, PA 19008-0914

http://www.chelseahouse.com

Contributing Editor: Isobel O'Donnell

CONTENTS

User's Guide

These volumes are designed to introduce the reader to the life and work of the world's literary masters. Each volume begins with Harold Bloom's essay "The Work in the Writer" and a volume-specific introduction also written by Professor Bloom. Following these unique introductions is an engaging biography that discusses the major life events and important literary accomplishments of the author under consideration.

Furthermore, each volume includes an original critique that not only traces the themes, symbols, and ideas apparent in the author's works, but strives to put those works into a cultural and historical perspectives. In addition to the original critique is a brief selection of significant critical essays previously published on the author and his or her works followed by a concise and informative chronology of the writer's life. Finally, each volume concludes with a bibliography of the writer's works, a list of additional readings, and an index of important themes and ideas.

The Work in the Writer

Literary biography found its masterpiece in James Boswell's *Life of Samuel Johnson*. Boswell, when he treated Johnson's writings, implicitly commented upon Johnson as found in his work, even as in the great critic's life. Modern instances of literary biography, such as Richard Ellmann's lives of W. B. Yeats, James Joyce, and Oscar Wilde, essentially follow in Boswell's pattern.

That the writer somehow is in the work, we need not doubt, though with William Shakespeare, writer-of-writers, we almost always need to rely upon pure surmise. The exquisite rancidities of the Problem Plays or Dark Comedies seem to express an extraordinary estrangement of Shakespeare from himself. When we read or attend *Troilus and Cressida* and *Measure for Measure*, we may be startled by particular speeches of Ulysses in the first play, or of Vincentio in the second. These speeches, of Ulysses upon hierarchy or upon time, or of Duke Vincentio upon death, are too strong either for their contexts or for the characters of their speakers. The same phenomenon occurs with Parolles, the military impostor of *All's Well That Ends Well*. Utterly disgraced, he nevertheless affirms: "Simply the thing I am/Shall make me live."

In Shakespeare, more even than in his peers, Dante and Cervantes, meaning always starts itself again through excess or overflow. The strongest of Shakespeare's creatures—Falstaff, Hamlet, Iago, Lear, Cleopatra—have an exuberance that is fiercer than their plays can contain. If Ben Jonson was at all correct in his complaint that "Shakespeare wanted art," it could have been only in a sense that he may not have intended. Where do the personalities of Falstaff or Hamlet touch a limit? What was it in Shakespeare that made the two parts of *Henry IV* and *Hamlet* into "plays unlimited"? Neither Falstaff nor Hamlet will be stopped: their wit, their beautiful, laughing speech, their intensity of being—all these are virtually infinite.

In what ways do Falstaff and Hamlet manifest the writer in the work? Evidently, we can never know, or know enough to answer with any authority. But what would happen if we reversed the question, and asked: How did the work form the writer, Shakespeare?

Of Shakespeare's inwardness, his biography tells us nothing. And yet, to an astonishing extent, Shakespeare created our inwardness. At the least, we can speculate that Shakespeare so lived his life as to conceal the depths of his nature, particularly as he rather prematurely aged. We do not have Shakespeare on Shakespeare, as any good reader of the Sonnets comes to realize: they do not constitute a key that unlocks his heart. No sequence of sonnets could be less confessional or more powerfully detached from the poet's self.

The German poet and universal genius, Goethe, affords a superb contrast to Shakespeare. Of Goethe's life, we know more than everything; I wonder sometimes if we know as much about Napoleon or Freud or any other human being who ever has lived, as we know about Goethe. Everywhere, we can find Goethe in his work, so much so that Goethe seems to crowd the writing out, just as Byron and Oscar Wilde seem to usurp their own literary accomplishments. Goethe, cunning beyond measure, nevertheless invested a rival exuberance in his greatest works that could match his personal charisma. The sublime outrageousness of the Second Part of *Faust*, or of the greater lyric and meditative poems, form a Counter-Sublime to Goethe's own daemonic intensity.

Goethe was fascinated by the daemonic in himself; we can doubt that Shakespeare had any such interests. Evidently, Shakespeare abandoned his acting career just before he composed *Measure for Measure* and *Othello*. I surmise that the egregious interventions by Vincentio and Iago displace the actor's energies into a new kind of mischief-making, a fresh opening to a subtler playwriting-within-the-play.

But what had opened Shakespeare to this new awareness? The answer is the work in the writer, *Hamlet* in Shakespeare. One can go further: it was not so much the play, *Hamlet*, as the character Hamlet, who changed Shakespeare's art forever.

Hamlet's personality is so large and varied that it rivals Goethe's own. Ironically Goethe's Faust, his Hamlet, has no personality at all, and is as colorless as Shakespeare himself seems to have chosen to be. Yet nothing could be more colorful than the Second Part of *Faust*, which is peopled by an astonishing array of monsters, grotesque devils and classical ghosts.

A contrast between Shakespeare and Goethe demonstrates that in each—but in very different ways—we can better find the work in the person, than we can discover that banal entity, the person in the work. Goethe to many of his contemporaries, seemed to be a mortal god. Shakespeare, so far as we know, seemed an affable, rather ordinary fellow, who aged early and became somewhat withdrawn. Yet Faust, though Mephistopheles battles for his soul, is hardly worth the trouble unless you take him as an idea and not as a person. Hamlet is nearly every-idea-in-one, but he is precisely a personality and a person.

Would Hamlet be so astonishingly persuasive if his father's ghost did not haunt him? Falstaff is more alive than Prince Hal, who says that the devil haunts him in the shape of an old fat man. Three years before composing the final *Hamlet*, Shakespeare invented Falstaff, who then never ceased to haunt his creator. Falstaff and Hamlet may be said to best represent the work in the writer, because their influence upon Shakespeare was prodigious. W.H. Auden accurately observed that Falstaff possesses infinite energy: never tired, never bored, and absolutely both witty and happy until Hal's rejection destroys him. Hamlet too has infinite energy, but in him it is more curse than blessing.

Falstaff and Hamlet can be said to occupy the roles in Shakespeare's invented world that Sancho Panza and Don Quixote possess in Cervantes's. Shakespeare's plays from 1610 on (starting with *Twelfth Night*) are thus analogous to the Second Part of Cervantes's epic novel. Sancho and the Don overtly jostle Cervantes for authorship in the Second Part, even as Cervantes battles against the impostor who has pirated a continuation of his work. As a dramatist, Shakespeare manifests the work in the writer more indirectly. Falstaff's prose genius is revived in the scapegoating of Malvolio by Maria and Sir Toby Belch, while Falstaff's darker insights are developed by Feste's melancholic wit. Hamlet's intellectual resourcefulness, already deadly, becomes poisonous in Iago and in Edmund. Yet we have not crossed into the deeper abysses of the work in the writer in later Shakespeare.

No fictive character, before or since, is Falstaff's equal in self-trust. Sir John, whose delight in himself is contagious, has total confidence both in his self-awareness and in the resources of his language. Hamlet, whose self is as strong, and whose language is as copious, nevertheless distrusts both the self and language. Later Shakespeare is, as it were, much under the influence both of Falstaff and of Hamlet, but they tug him in opposite directions. Shakespeare's own copiousness of language is well-nigh incredible: a vocabulary in excess of twenty-one thousand words, almost eighteen hundred of which he coined himself. And of his word-hoard, nearly half are used only once each, as though the perfect setting for each had been found, and need not be repeated. Love for language and faith in language are Falstaffian attributes. Hamlet will darken both that love and that faith in Shakespeare, and perhaps the Sonnets can best be read as Falstaff and Hamlet counterpointing against one another.

Can we surmise how aware Shakespeare was of Falstaff and Hamlet, once they had played themselves into existence? *Henry IV, Part I* appeared in six quarto editions during Shakespeare's lifetime; *Hamlet* possibly had four. Falstaff and Hamlet were played again and again at the Globe, but Shakespeare knew also that they were being read, and he must have had contact with some of those readers. What would it have been like to discuss Falstaff or Hamlet with one of their early readers (presumably also part of their audience at the Globe), if you were the creator of such demiurges? The question would seem nonsensical to most Shakespeare scholars, but then these days they tend to be either ideologues or moldy figs. How can we recover the uncanniness of Falstaff and of Hamlet, when they now have become so familiar?

A writer's influence upon himself is an unexplored problem in criticism, but such an influence is never free from anxieties. The biocritical problem (which this series attempts to explore) can be divided into two areas, difficult to disengage fully. Accomplished works affect the author's life, and also affect her subsequent writings. It is simpler for me to surmise the effect of *Mrs. Dalloway* and *To the Lighthouse* upon Woolf's late *Between the Acts*, than it is to relate Clarissa Dalloway's suicide and Lily Briscoe's capable endurance in art to the tragic death and complex life of Virginia Woolf.

There are writers whose lives were so vivid that they seem sometimes to obscure the literary achievement: Byron, Wilde, Malraux, Hemingway. But most major Western writers do not live that exuberantly, and the greatest of all, Shakespeare, sometimes appears to have adopted the personal mask of colorlessness. And yet there are heroes of literature who struggled titanically with their own eras—Tolstoy, Milton, Victor Hugo—who nevertheless matter more for their works than their lives.

There are great figures—Emily Dickinson, Wallace Stevens, Willa Cather—who seem to have had so little of the full intensity of life when compared to the vitality of their work, that we might almost speak of the work in the work, rather than even of the work in a person. Emily Brontë might well be the extreme instance of such a visionary, surpassing William Blake in that one regard.

I conclude this general introduction to a series of literary bio-critiques by stating a tentative formula or principle for gauging the many ways in which the work influences the person and her subsequent, later work. Our influence upon ourselves is always related to the Shakespearean invention of self-overhearing, which I have written about in several other contexts. Life, as well as poetry and prose, is overheard rather than simply heard. The writer listens to herself as though she were somebody else, and the will to change begins to operate. The forces that live in us include the prior work we have done, and the dreams and waking visions that evade our dismissals.

HAROLD BLOOM

Introduction

Where, in Hemingway, can we best locate the work in the writer? As with Lord Byron, Oscar Wilde, Norman Mailer, there is never any problem locating the writer in the work, in Hemingway's instance. More people have a recognition of the Hemingway myth than have ever read Hemingway. He lives on in the public imagination as Papa, the hard-drinking big-game hunter, war correspondent and pugilist (he literally knocked down Wallace Stevens, and figuratively hoped he could go fifteen rounds with Leo Tolstoy). We associate him with Paris in the 1920s, Madrid in the 1930s, and after that a blend of Havana and Key West, until he went home to emulate his father's suicide.

It is in *The Nick Adams Stories*, collected as a single volume in 1972, eleven years after Hemingway's death, that I think we encounter most fully the work in the writer, the influence of the poet upon himself. I say "poet" deliberately, echoing Wallace Stevens, for whom Hemingway was essentially a poet, whose subject was "extraordinary actuality." I do not mean that we are to read the Nick Adams stories as prose-poems, though the strongest among them are stylistic masterpieces: "The Light of the World," "The Killers," "In Another Country," "Big Two-Hearted River," and "The End of Something." But these are also sustained visions, which is rare in short stories. They, even "The Killers," are Hemingway's portraits of the artist as a young man, Nick Adams.

Eight—mostly unfinished—Nick Adams stories, that Hemingway did not publish, are marvelous revelations both of the writer's stylistic art, and the sometimes invidious effects of Hemingway's own work upon him. In a

1

clear sense, he was his own worst influence, as here in "On Writing," where something unruly breaks loose:

> Talking about anything was bad. Writing about anything actual was bad. It always killed it.
>
> The only writing that was any good was what you made up, what you imagined. That made everything come true. Like when he wrote "My Old Man" he'd never seen a jockey killed and the next week Georges Parfrement was killed at that very jump and that was the way it looked. Everything good he'd ever written he'd made up. None of it had ever happened. Other things had happened. Better things, maybe. That was what the family couldn't understand. They thought it all was experience.
>
> That was the weakness of Joyce. Daedalus in *Ulysses* was Joyce himself, so he was terrible. Joyce was so damn romantic and intellectual about him. He'd made Bloom up, Bloom was wonderful. He'd made Mrs. Bloom up. She was the greatest in the world.
>
> That was the way with Mac. Mac worked too close to life. You had to digest life and then create your own people. Mac had stuff, though.
>
> Nick in the stories was never himself. He made him up. Of course he'd never seen an Indian woman having a baby. That was what made it good. Nobody knew that. He'd seen a woman have a baby on the road to Karagatch and tried to help her. That was the way it was.
>
> He wished he could always write like that. He would sometime. He wanted to be a great writer. He was pretty sure he would be. He knew it in lots of ways. He would in spite of everything. It was hard, though.
>
> It was hard to be a great writer if you loved the world and living in it and special people. It was hard when you loved so many places. Then you were healthy and felt good and were having a good time and what the hell.

"In the presence of extraordinary actuality, consciousness takes the place of imagination" is one of the *Adagia* of Wallace Stevens. Who judges what is extraordinary? I know nothing either of trout-fishing or of bullfighting, but sometimes when Hemingway writes about trout-fishing, I am persuaded of what Emerson linked as "the transcendental and extraordinary." Bull-fighting, doubtless a skill, a sport, an art to entire national cultures, is the center of Hemingway's *Death in the Afternoon*, which I assume gratifies a special taste I cannot share. As a literary critic, Hemingway is properly defensive; the short stories of *Dubliners* share an eminence with Hemingway's, Chekhov's, and only a few others. But you are ill-advised to reread even *The Sun Also Rises*, the best of Hemingway's novels, side-by-side with rereading *Ulysses*. Stephen wanes in the presence of Leopold Bloom, but Jake Barnes is only a name upon a page when compared with Daedalus. Joyce had and hadn't made Poldy up; Poldy was the Portrait of the Artist as a Middle-aged Man, as Richard Ellmann demonstrates in his biography of Joyce. Whether Molly "was the greatest in the world" is rather disputable, but beyond argument her substance is more an achieved representation than is that of Lady Brett Ashley. One isn't using Joyce as a club against Hemingway; the point is to surmise why Hemingway goes so bad whenever he goes bad. Joyce parodies an aspect of himself in the Stephen of *Ulysses*; Hemingway's self-parodies are involuntary, as in the passage quoted above.

Much more interesting because it is so poignant is the long, puzzling "The Last Good Country," where the work in the writer, Nick Adams in Ernest Hemingway, traps the reader into seventy pages that alternate between narrative incoherence and stylistic brilliance. The incoherence has little to do with the status of incompleteness scholars defensively assert for "The Last Good Country." Plot isn't the problem; an incremental tension or inconsistency between character and style is troublesome, and may account for Hemingway's abandonment of what could have been a remarkable novella, closer to *The Adventures of Huckleberry Finn* than anything else by Hemingway, even the marvelous "Big Two-Hearted River."

Two game wardens, one of them potentially dangerous, come after Nick Adams because he has killed a deer out of season. Hemingway is not much interested in the wardens, and so they bore us at some length, in the middle part of the story, taking up pages 92-107 of *The Nick Adams Stories*. The life of "The Last Good Country" is the adventures out in the open woods of Nick and his twelve-year-old youngest sister, called Littless. In the mode of Shakespearean pastoral comedy, Littless has cut off her hair to look like a boy, in order to join Nick in his flight from the law. Alas, both Nick and Littless have been reading Hemingway, and their conversational exchanges can be charmingly improbable:

> "I like it," Nick said. "The hell with everything. I like it very much."
>
> "Thank you, Nickie, so much. I was laying trying to rest like you said. But all I could do was imagine things to do for you. I was going to get you a chewing tobacco can full of knockout

drops from some big saloon in some place like Sheboygan."

"Who did you get them from?"

Nick was sitting down now and his sister sat on his lap and held her arms around his neck and rubbed her cropped head against his cheek.

"I got them from the Queen of the Whores," she said. "And you know that name of the saloon?"

"No."

"The Royal Ten Dollar Gold Piece Inn and Emporium."

"What did you do there?"

"I was a whore's assistant."

"What's a whore's assistant do?"

"Oh she carries the whore's train when she walks and opens her carriage door and shows her to the right room. It's like a lady in waiting I guess."

"What's she say to the whore?"

"She'll say anything that comes into her mind as long as it's polite."

"Like what, brother?"

"Like, 'Well ma'am, it must be pretty tiring on a hot day like today to be just a bird in a gilded cage.' Things like that."

"What's the whore say?"

"She says, 'Yes indeedy. It sure is sweetness.' Because this whore I was whore's assistant to is of humble origin."

"What kind of origin are you?"

"I'm the sister or the brother of a morbid writer and I'm delicately brought up. This makes me intensely desirable to the main whore and to all of her circle."

Littless is not only Hemingwayesque, but amiably incestuous in desiring her brother, who is somewhat wary of the possibility. As a Hemingway parodist, Littless is hard to beat, as here when she thinks of emulating Jael in the Book of Judges, hammering spikes into the temples of the sleeping game wardens:

"What were you going to do?" he asked again. Littless leaned forward and spat toward the grill.

"How was that?"

"You missed the skillet anyway."

"Oh, it's pretty bad. I got it out of the Bible. I was going to take three spikes, one for each of them, and drive them into the temples of those two and that boy while they slept."

"What were you going to drive them in with?"

"A muffled hammer."

"How do you muffle a hammer?"

"I'd muffle it all right."

"That nail thing's pretty rough to try."

"Well, that girl did it in the Bible and since I've seen armed men drunk and asleep and circulated among them at night and stolen their whiskey why shouldn't I go the whole way, especially if I learned it in the Bible?"

"They didn't have a muffled hammer in the Bible."

"I guess I mixed it up with muffled oars."

"Maybe. And we don't want to kill anybody. That's why you came along."

"I know. But crime comes easy for you and me, Nickie. We're different from the others. Then I thought if I was ruined morally I might as well be useful."

You can yield to this and be delighted, but Littless is excessive even as parody. Essentially, this is Hemingway's version of a Shakespearean comedy routine, but it rings wrong in: "How do you muffle a hammer?" and "why shouldn't I go the whole way, especially if I learned it in the Bible?" We are listening to an incestuous love-song, rather than to an adventure story:

He loved his sister very much and she loved him too much. But, he thought, I guess these things straighten out. At least I hope so.

Perhaps "The Last Good Country" did not get finished because palpably Littless has no intention of letting things straighten out:

"Thank you for putting the Mackinaw on me. Wasn't it a lovely night, though?"

"Yes. Did you sleep all night?"

"I'm still asleep. Nickie, can we stay here always?"

"I don't think so. You'd grow up and have to get married."

"I'm going to get married to you anyway. I want to be your common-law wife. I read about it in the paper."

"That's where you read about the Unwritten Law."

"Sure. I'm going to be your common-law wife under the Unwritten Law. Can't I, Nickie?"

"No."

"I will. I'll surprise you. All you have to do is live a certain time as man and wife. I'll get them to count this time now. It's just like homesteading."

"I won't let you file."

"You can't help yourself. That's the Unwritten Law. I've thought it out lots of times. I'll get cards printed Mrs. Nick Adams, Cross Village, Michigan—common-law wife. I'll hand these out to a few people openly each year until the time's up."

"I don't think it would work."

"I've got another scheme. We'll have a couple of children while I'm a minor. Then you have to marry me under the Unwritten law."

"That's not the Unwritten Law."

"I get mixed up on it."

"Anyway, nobody knows yet if it works."

Littless begins to seem more and more to have emerged from some wickedly delicious fairytale, but "The Last Good Country"'s authentic orgy is Hemingway's prose exfoliating outrageously:

They went along down the creek. Nick was studying the banks. He had seen a mink's track and shown it to his sister and they had seen tiny ruby-crowned kinglets that were hunting insects and let the boy and girl come close as they moved sharply and delicately in the cedars. They had seen cedar waxwings so calm and gentle and distinguished moving in their lovely elegance with the magic wax touches on their wing coverts and their tails, and Littless had said, "They're the most beautiful, Nickie. There couldn't be more simply beautiful birds."

"They're built like your face," he said.

"No, Nickie. Don't make fun. Cedar waxwings make me so proud and happy that I cry."

"When they wheel and light and then move so proud and friendly and gently," Nick said.

This is very high rhetoric indeed, but not good training to go fifteen rounds with Count Leo Tolstoy. The influence of Hemingway upon Hemingway became overwhelming, and the work in the writer triumphed over the writer's work.

VEDA BOYD JONES

Biography of Ernest Hemingway

THE TIME OF HOPE

Paris—that wonderful old city held such hope. If Ernest Hemingway wanted to be a writer, then that's where he should be, author Sherwood Anderson told him. Paris was where a young man could study modern writing. Paris was where a young man could make valuable contacts. Paris was where a young man could make it as a writer.

Hemingway met Anderson at a friend's apartment in Chicago in 1921 and took the older man's advice to heart. A few months later, twenty-two-year-old Hemingway packed up his unfinished novel about World War I, a few poems, and some short stories.

In December 1921, he and his new wife, Hadley, boarded a ship for Paris. On the journey, Hemingway's exuberance knew no limits. He sang, he shouted, and he dreamed about his new life. Once in Paris, armed with introductory letters from Anderson to influential people, the couple checked into an inexpensive hotel.

Here he was, in an old world-city that was brand new to him. Hemingway bought a guide book, and the newlyweds explored. They walked on cobblestone streets, drank wine at cafés, and watched the people all around them.

The city didn't comprise only native-born Frenchmen, Paris was renowned for drawing philosophers, radicals, and expatriates alike. It was a city where a prim and proper upbringing often gave way to wild and exciting times. Although Prohibition was in force in the United States the

Hemingways had left behind, wine and drink flowed at Paris bars. Strict sexual morals from home were disdained by a free and impulsive expatriate society. This accepting of the unacceptable was a feeling in the air, and Hemingway took it all in.

Hadley had studied French in school, and at first she spoke for her husband in halting French. Hemingway listened carefully and read English and French newspaper accounts of the same stories, noting how key words translated. He quickly picked up Parisian slang, although he never mastered correct grammar, and his remarkable memory allowed him to communicate in French in a short time.

Still, there were many times when his English was enough. Within a few days, Hemingway walked into Shakespeare and Company, a bookstore owned by Sylvia Beach, formerly of New Jersey. He presented her with one of Anderson's letters of introduction. In it, Anderson had graciously called Hemingway "a writer instinctively in touch with everything worthwhile" and said the Hemingways were "delightful people to know."

Sylvia Beach's store was also a rental library. For a small fee Hemingway could check out two volumes at a time. Furthermore, Beach's place was also an entry into expatriate life. On cold winter days the stove was often surrounded by writers and artists discussing literary and intellectual topics. Beach was a helpful woman, who loaned money to those in need, collected mail for those off on holiday, and mediated colorful arguments among her patrons. Hemingway remembered her in his memoirs, *A Moveable Feast*, as the person who treated him the nicest of anyone he'd ever known:

> Sylvia had a lively, sharply sculptured face, brown eyes that were as alive as a small animal's and as gay as a young girl's, and wavy brown hair that was brushed back from her fine forehead and cut thick below her ears and at the line of the collar of the brown velvet jacket she wore. She had pretty legs and she was kind, cheerful and interested, and loved to make jokes and gossip.

By the second week of January, the Hemingways had found a fourth-floor walk-up apartment. It was in the oldest part of the Left Bank: 74 rue du Cardinal Lemoine. Hemingway wrote his parents that it was:

> the jolliest place you ever saw. We rented it furnished for 250 francs a month, about 18 dollars… Bones [Hadley] has a piano and we have all our pictures up on the walls and an open fire place and a peach of a kitchen and a dining room and big bed room and dressing room and plenty of space. It is on top of a

high hill in the very oldest part of Paris. The nicest part of the Latin Quarter.

His description of the apartment was less than accurate and demonstrates the fictionist in Hemingway—even in letters. The two-room apartment was tiny. Hadley's piano dominated the dining room and forced them to move the table into the living-bedroom. Only one person could stand in the kitchen appendage that held a two-burner stove. The shared bathroom was at the end of the hall by the stairs.

As soon as the Hemingways had moved into their Paris apartment, they departed for Switzerland. A flu epidemic gripped Paris, and Hemingway was already suffering with a sore throat. Out of the rainy Paris weather and into the dry powder snow of Switzerland, his health revived, and he and Hadley had a holiday of bobsledding.

The trip abroad was financed by Hadley's trust fund and supplemented by Hemingway's income as a European correspondent for the *Toronto Star* newspaper. Although he had come to Paris to write fiction, he found that it was easier to write newspaper articles. Journalism was part of his education in writing.

As soon as the Hemingways returned to Paris in February, they sent Anderson's letter of introduction to Ezra Pound, formerly of Idaho. Pound, a poet and literary talent scout for magazines, invited Hemingway and his wife to tea.

Hemingway's first impression of Pound—sandy red hair, patchy beard, and sporting a pince-nez—was not favorable. Pound seemed too pompous, too artsy, too affected. But soon Pound became a surrogate father to Hemingway and offered him the best advice for a writer. Read. Read. Read.

Pound listed authors who were absolute musts. Of course, there were T.S. Eliot, James Joyce and Henry James, but Pound directed Hemingway to the classics as well—Homer, Chaucer, Dante, and Donne. Pound read some of Hemingway's works and drilled into him that cutting, revising, and rewriting were necessary for tight prose. Be specific. Do not write in the abstract. Use no extra words. Make scenes believable. Write what you know.

Pound thought of Hemingway as another of his literary finds, and he sent some of Hemingway's poems to the literary magazine, *Dial*. The poems were rejected, and the rejection smacked Hemingway in the face. *Dial* routinely published the work of Sherwood Anderson, who had so kindly written those introductory letters. Competitive Hemingway wanted to write better than Anderson, and he desperately wanted to see his work in print.

Hemingway didn't like the sit-around-and-talk world of the writers who hung around the cafés. He didn't want to be included in what he saw as an effeminate crowd. He wanted action and he wanted writing—an odd combination in Paris. So he taught Pound to box, and the duo played tennis. Still, these physical workouts were peppered with conversations on writing. Hemingway took it all in, and he was a very quick study.

But Pound wasn't his only writing teacher. In March, Hemingway mailed Anderson's introductory letter to Gertrude Stein of Pennsylvania, expatriate head of art and literature circles in Paris and champion of the modernist movement. Stein immediately asked the Hemingways to tea at the apartment she shared with Alice Toklas.

The Hemingways admired the paintings by Cezanne, Picasso, and Matisse, which lined Stein's salon walls, and then they took tea near the big fireplace. Stein spoke to Hemingway while Toklas conversed with Hadley. Hemingway remembered the meeting:

> Miss Stein was very big but not tall and was heavily built like a peasant woman. She had beautiful eyes and a strong German-Jewish face that also could have been Friulano and she reminded me of a northern Italian peasant woman with her clothes, her mobile face and her lovely, thick, alive immigrant hair which she wore put up in the same way she had probably worn it in college. She talked all the time and at first it was about people and places.

The Hemingways accepted the Stein-Toklas lesbian relationship and invited the couple to their cramped apartment for tea. At the appointed time, Stein laboriously waddled up the stairs and installed herself on the bed. She read Hemingway's short story "Up in Michigan" and declared it not publishable because of the sexual explicitness. After reading a bit of the uncompleted novel he had started in Chicago, she said, "Begin over again and concentrate."

Stein became Hemingway's surrogate mother. She was much like his own mother, whom he disliked. She was large, talented, strong-willed, and didn't apologize for her opinions or her way of life. Stein told Hemingway to quit newspaper work because he wouldn't be able to see things; he'd just see words, and that would never make him a real writer.

Hemingway regularly visited the Stein salon, and she critiqued other manuscripts for him. He read Stein's *Three Lives* and learned her style of repetition, verbal connections, and alliteration.

Stein's literary technique was free association and many times it lacked sense to Hemingway, but her use of the present tense was a way of getting started. He used this technique as his shorthand method of taking notes on people, places, and things he observed. He began writing in blue notebooks, the same as Stein. But he didn't take all of her words as gold. She didn't rewrite and believed that the first draft was the best way and the only way in free association.

Hemingway took what he thought was right from Stein's methods, took what he thought was right from Ezra Pound's methods, and added them to his own innate style. He worked on his prose when time allowed. But newspaper work interfered with his fiction, and he was not yet at a place where he could take Stein's advice and give up journalism.

The *Toronto Star* asked Hemingway to go to the International Economic Conference in Genoa. In April 1922, Hemingway took the train to Italy. He knew little about European economic conditions, except that it was cheap to live in Europe, because the American dollar held up very well. His first reports were features on the conference delegates. As he hung around with fellow reporters, he picked up their knowledge of economics and wrote some insightful pieces. He also picked up their command of short pithy sentences, which were necessary for sending terse cables back to their newspapers.

Tired after his work in Genoa, Hemingway returned to Paris at the end of April. A month later, he and Hadley left for a hiking trip in Switzerland and into Italy. They retraced Hemingway's steps in World War I and tried to locate the place where he'd been wounded, but everything had changed. The trenches were gone, the land was green again, and Hemingway found he couldn't go back. He had only his memories. And if he didn't have notes on this time, right now, then he could not recapture this very moment. It was another writing lesson learned.

When the couple returned to Paris in mid-June, Hemingway read, wrote, and watched horse races with Hadley on spring afternoons. He took notes on everything around him.

His literary aspects were looking up, giving him great hope. A New Orleans magazine, *Double Dealer*, had published a short, satirical fable in the May issue and a poem in the June issue, both written before he crossed the Atlantic. The editor was a friend of Sherwood Anderson's, and Hemingway understood that it was a who-you-know-world.

Also that summer, *Poetry* magazine of Chicago accepted the six poems that the *Dial* had rejected. Ezra Pound's name had influenced the editor to read the poems, but they were accepted on their own merit.

Buoyed by his successes, Hemingway wrote a new short story, "My Old Man," about a boy's disappointment in his father, a famous jockey. He used his observations at the racetrack for the background, and what he didn't know he imagined and researched enough to make it believable.

With plenty to celebrate, Hemingway and Hadley again left Paris, this time for an August walking tour of the Black Forest of Germany with friends. Hemingway and Hadley flew on a relatively new airline to Strasbourg, France. Bill Bird, a newsman Hemingway had palled around with in Genoa, and his wife refused to fly and rode the ten-hour train journey to Strasbourg, where they hooked up with the Hemingways and another couple. Hemingway wrote about the two-and-a-half-hour plane flight for the *Star*. He had learned to write about his own experiences.

Back in Paris in September, Hemingway had time to read in the papers about the growing unrest between Greece and Turkey. Soon the *Star* asked him to go to Constantinople to cover the war. At the same time, the International News Service asked him to report on the war. Although he was under exclusive contract to the *Star*, Hemingway rationalized that the *Star* wanted features and INS wanted news. He could do both. He spent over two weeks in Constantinople, working hard. When the *Star* editor complained that the wire service had, word-for-word, the same stories that Hemingway had sent him, Hemingway patched things up by saying they had been stolen.

Upon his return to Paris, Hemingway learned that Bill Bird's hand-set press, that he'd bought as a hobby, was now Three Mountains Press and would print his first book. Erza Pound had agreed to edit six short books of essays, poems, and stories. He'd lined up other authors who had a backlog of material to publish. Hemingway didn't know what should go in his book, so it was listed as *Blank* on the promotional sheet.

He wrote *Poetry* magazine, asking if those six poems could be reprinted. He thought "My Old Man" was good enough for the book. He had some short sketches of people in his file, and he had the beginning of a story on fishing. He was still pondering what to include when he was sent to Switzerland to cover the Lausanne Conference for two Hearst wire services. Hadley was to go with him, but she came down with a horrible cold.

A couple weeks later, Hadley was able to travel and boarded the train to Lausanne. So that Hemingway could work on his material, she had put his three folders of manuscripts in a small suitcase. A porter carried her luggage to her compartment, but during the time it was out of her sight, the small suitcase was stolen.

When Hemingway met her at the train station, she could not speak through her sobs. When he finally coaxed the story out of her, he couldn't believe it. Surely she hadn't brought all three folders—the manuscripts, the typed copies, *and* the carbons. He immediately took the night train back to Paris to look for himself.

The shelf was empty. Stuck away in a drawer was a copy of "Up in Michigan" that Stein had said was unpublishable. "My Old Man" had been sent to a magazine, so he would have that returned copy. He'd sent one chapter of the fishing story to a friend, and the six poems were in that magazine, so he could retrieve them. But the unfinished novel was gone.

When Ezra Pound heard of the loss, he called it "an act of Gawd." He told Hemingway that "no one is *known* to have lost anything by *suppression* of early work." If there was a good foundation for a story, then Hemingway could recreate it.

His first year in Paris, the year of hope, had yielded little in the way of manuscripts, but it had been the equivalent of a college education in writing.

Now Ernest Hemingway could start again and this time make a big name for himself.

CHILDHOOD OF WONDER

Ernest Miller Hemingway was born July 21, 1899, in Oak Park, Illinois, an upper middle-class suburb of Chicago. His father, Clarence, was a doctor, and his mother, Grace, was a music teacher. Both were followers of the Congregational Church, and they expected their offspring to adhere to their strict religious beliefs.

Clarence was an outdoorsman and had a deep affection for fishing, hunting, camping, and hiking. In college, he played football. Fascinated by Indian culture, he collected artifacts dug out of nearby mounds. One of his great memories was the geological expedition he and male friends once made in the Great Smoky Mountains of North Carolina. Clarence had a deep desire to help mankind, and in that service he gave medical care to those who could not afford it and started a club, which taught nature appreciation and hygiene to young boys. He instilled a love of the outdoors in his son.

Grace Hall Hemingway at one time wanted to be an opera singer. She made her debut at Madison Square Garden in New York City, but the glare of the stage lights hurt her eyes, which had been damaged in childhood by scarlet fever, and she gave up the stage. Instead of a career as a diva, for which her temperament was well suited, she taught voice lessons, and for many years her annual income was greater than her husband's. A big woman, talented and creative, she tended to rule the Hemingway home. Her mother had told her, "There is no use any woman getting into the kitchen if she can help it," and that early lesson was taken to heart by Grace. Her husband did most of the cooking. She required servants to help in the house and regularly needed time alone away from her family.

Ernest was eighteen months younger than his sister, Marcelline, but Grace had an odd habit of dressing the two alike and passing them off as twins. Later, Marcelline was held back from school so they could both enter first grade together. In their toddler years, the duo sometimes wore dresses and sometimes wore overalls. They both played with stick guns and dolls.

But Ernest showed at a young age that he wanted to be all male. When asked what he was afraid of, he'd shout, "Fraid a nothing." As a child he'd throw a fit, screaming and yelling when he was not given his own way, sometimes slapping those who defied him, then later kissing them and saying he was sorry.

He loved looking at picture books, and his favorites were the bound volumes of the monthly serial *Birds of Nature*. Before he was two years old, he astounded his mother by successfully naming 73 birds by looking at their pictures.

His imagination knew no bounds. After seeing a Wild West show, he pretended to be Pawnee Bill. After seeing a circus, he pulled a little wagon and pretended it was a circus cart bearing animals. When he was five, he told his grandfather that he had single-handedly stopped a runaway horse. Grandfather Hall told his daughter that Ernest "is going to be heard from some day. If he uses his imagination for good purposes, he'll be famous, but if he starts the wrong way, with all his energy, he'll end in jail, and it's up to you which way he goes."

Each summer, the Hemingways went north to their cottage, called Windemere, on the shores of Walloon Lake in Michigan. The house had no electricity, no indoor bathrooms, and the two bedrooms were soon crowded. By the summer of 1905, Ernest had three sisters, and he desperately wanted a brother. For male companionship, he befriended boys in the area, and they ran in the fields, rowed in the boat, and fished in the creeks.

School was tolerable to Ernest, and he was a fast learner, but he yearned for the freedom of summers in Michigan. When his father would join the family up north for his short vacation from his medical practice, he would take Ernest hunting. Ernest's poor eyesight never let him match the shooting skill of his father, although he became a pretty good shot at flying game.

Two days before his twelfth birthday, Ernest got yet another sister. Grandfather Hemingway gave him a more appreciated gift—a 20-gauge shotgun. Accompanying the gift were lessons on what to shoot and what not to shoot. Ernest's father believed that wild game was for eating. Vermin could be shot because they killed chickens, but he would not allow the shooting of just any animal for sport.

In 1913, Ernest and Marcelline started high school. In his freshman year, Ernest was embarrassed by his height—a half-foot shorter than his sister. That summer his growth spurt started, and he grew at the rate of an inch a month. During his sophomore year, he played a cello in the school orchestra and hiked miles with the hiking club. During this year, he got the long-awaited brother, but it was years too late for little Leicester Hemingway to be the playmate Ernest had yearned for.

Still, Hemingway had plenty of male friends to take the place of brothers. The summer before his junior year, he and a friend traveled up to Michigan on a ship, then hiked and hitched rides the final 100 miles to Walloon Lake. The boys camped out and ate trout they caught at various streams. Once at Windemere, they took the shutters off the windows and aired the cottage for the arrival of the rest of the family.

Ernest spent the summer hiking, hunting, fishing, visiting with friends, working in the garden, and helping with the haying. He had bulked up during the summer, and after returning to school, boxing caught his interest. He observed boxers at some Chicago gyms, but his workouts were mostly in his mother's large music room and against boys smaller than he. A bully streak in his personality let him enjoy pummeling his opponent.

Hemingway wrote a story about a boxing match, which appeared in the April issue of the school's literary magazine, *Tabula*. His first short story, dealing with hunting and suicide, had appeared two months earlier. At the same time he was writing fiction, Hemingway was reporting for the school newspaper, *The Trapeze*.

The summer before his senior year, Hemingway again set out with a friend for Windemere Cottage. They encountered friendly folk along the way, and Hemingway recorded details of people and events in his diary. He jotted down that he had killed a water moccasin on the railroad track, he had traded fish he'd caught for milk, and he had hiked to Rapid River and fished the fastest running stream he'd ever seen.

His senior year in high school, Hemingway continued to write for *The Trapeze* and submitted one story to *Tabula*. After two years of sitting on the bench for the lightweight football team, he had finally beefed up enough to try out for the first team. Still, he was awkward and played just enough to earn a letter. He swam on the swimming team, but he found he preferred individual activities like fishing and hunting to team sports.

As a tribute to his writing skills, he was named class prophet for the graduating class. His narrative about class members was the highlight of the assembly on Class Day. And then his formal education was over.

Ernest could have gone to Oberlin College with Marcelline, but that path didn't interest him. His father thought he was too young to sign up for the military, as some of his classmates had done now that the United States had joined the fighting in the First World War, so Ernest ruled out that option. With connections through his uncle in Kansas City, Ernest learned that there would be reporter jobs opening in the fall at the *Star*. That's what he wanted—a journalism job. And the delay in employment meant one last wonderful summer at Windemere.

The summer of 1917 didn't go quite as young Hemingway had planned. He worked hard in the hay fields and the garden, but he grew rebellious. He was tired of his father's strict rules, tired of his mother's selfish ways, tired of his father's kowtowing to his mother's stronger will. While his mother was on a short trip, his father wrote her that Ernest "is just as headstrong and abusive and threatening as ever."

The prospect of being away from his parents' control and being on his own appealed greatly, and with huge relief he boarded the train for Kansas City in October. His uncle met him at the station and the following day took him to the *Star*'s newsroom and introduced him to a friend. With the shortage of reporters caused by the draft, Hemingway was immediately hired at $15 a week with a thirty-day trial period.

In the enormous newsroom, old battered desks stood in long rows. The noise from voices, clattering typewriters, and ringing telephones was thrilling and exciting. Hemingway was taken to a desk. He sat down on the desktop and grinned. Here he was, a rookie reporter on a big city newspaper—just where he wanted to be.

He reported directly to assistant city editor C. G. "Pete" Wellington, who explained the type of writing demanded at the newspaper—simple declarative sentences. He gave Hemingway the *Star* style sheet with its 110 items including, "Use short sentences. Use short first paragraphs. Use vigorous English, not forgetting to strive for smoothness. Be positive, not negative." Hemingway later said they were "the best rules I ever learned for the business of writing. I've never forgotten them."

His beat was called the 'short stop run.' He covered the police station on Fifteenth Street, Union Station, and the general hospital. His hours were eight to five with Sunday off, but he was out in the field during most of that time. He was notorious for failing to keep in touch with the newsroom. Wellington said, "When we would put in a call for him at the hospital, we would learn that he had gone out on an ambulance call. He seemed always to want to be wherever the action was."

Within a short while, Hemingway moved from his uncle's house to an apartment he shared with an older friend he'd met in Michigan. Other than his hiking trips to Windemere Cottage, this was Hemingway's first taste of freedom away from a relative's judging eyes. He quickly fell away from the church, but told his parents that he didn't attend because he routinely worked until the wee hours on Sunday morning to get the Sunday edition out. After a couple of months with his friend, he rented a tiny apartment of his very own.

He hung out at bars with the older reporters on the *Star*. He once got into a fight and punched out a man who had been bullying a friend. His fist went through a glass cigar case and required bandaging. With his white badge of courage, Hemingway enjoyed hero status for a few days.

One reporter caught Hemingway's interest as a hard-boiled, hard-drinking, hard-fighting male. He wrote a sketch of the reporter:

> Lionel Moise was a great rewrite man. He could carry four stories in his head and go to the telephone and take a fifth and then write all five at full speed to catch an edition. There would be something alive about each one. He was always the highest paid man on every paper he worked on. ... He never spoke to the other reporters unless he had been drinking. He was tall and thick and had long arms and big hands. He was the fastest man on a typewriter I ever knew.

Had Hemingway been able to look into his future, he might have seen himself in this description. The two writers may have resembled in actions, but their writing was not the same. As Moise pointed out years later, "Like all real writers, he owes his well-deserved eminence not to any 'influence' but to his ability to select from a host of influences—part of that little thing called genius."

Hemingway talked with other reporters and asked how they got their stories and how they wrote them. He listened, and he wrote, wrote, wrote. He took on extra assignments from editor Charles Hopkins of the morning *Times*, which was put out by the same publisher as the *Star*. Hopkins liked Hemingway's work and told him, "Don't let anyone ever say that you were 'taught' writing. It was born in you."

Also born in him was an interest in military activities. He joined the Home Guard not long after he arrived in Kansas City and regularly reported for practice drills and maneuvers. He proudly wore a regular army olive drab uniform with the special black and gold hat cord of Missouri.

With the arrival at the *Star* of new employee Ted Brumback, Hemingway learned of adventures in Europe that he was missing. Ted had joined the American Field Service as an ambulance driver and had served for four months in France. The Red Cross was looking for ambulance drivers, but Ted said it would be best to drive in spring instead of in winter when rain turned the roads to muck. The two signed up for duty when Italian Red Cross officials were in Kansas City on a recruitment trip early in the new year, 1918.

Ernest's father gave his blessing to this venture feeling it would be a Christian way of helping the war effort without fighting.

His on-the-job-training as a journalist ended after six months with the *Star*, but Hemingway had filled every minute. He drew his last paycheck in April and headed for a brief visit home. He enjoyed a last trip to Windemere Cottage with friends before heading across the Atlantic.

THE WAR EXPERIENCE

As a recruit for the Red Cross, Hemingway was required to pass a physical in New York. He passed with a B rating, but his vision was so bad, the examining doctor suggested he get glasses. Hemingway ignored this advice. He was then given the rank of honorary second lieutenant and a regular U.S. Army officer's uniform with red enamel crosses on the cap and collar. Hemingway wrote a friend that regular army noncommissioned officers and privates were required to salute "Honorary First Lieuts" as Hemingway promoted himself and others in the rescue service. On a walk down Broadway, he claimed he was saluted 367 times.

On May 17, 1918, he marched in a parade along with 75,000 men and women to launch a Red Cross fund drive. Hemingway said "by virtue of his manly form and perfect complexion" he was placed in the right guide position of the first platoon. When the eyes-right command was given at a viewing platform, he got a good look at President Woodrow Wilson, who had traveled to New York to support the cause.

Six days later Hemingway boarded the ship *Chicago* for passage to Europe. Except for one storm, which found him sick and heaving over the rails with other passengers, the cruise was as smooth as his many boating experiences on Walloon Lake.

Once in France, his group was transported by train to Paris. Here was the excitement Hemingway had longed for. A long-range German gun regularly bombarded the city with explosive shells. Hemingway and his buddy Ted Brumback hired a taxi to drive them around the city following the sounds of bursting shells. When one exploded nearby, Hemingway decided it was time to retire to the hotel, out of range of the gun.

A few days later Hemingway was at work in Milan, Italy. He wrote his former coworkers at the Kansas City *Star* that he "had my first baptism of fire my first day here when an entire munitions factory exploded." His job was to gather up bodies, and he was unprepared for the sight. These fatalities were women, and body parts were scattered everywhere. His first brush with the mutilation of war made a lasting impression.

Two days later, Hemingway was sent to Schio, Italy. As part of American Red Cross Section Four he lived in an abandoned factory building, which the men dubbed the Schio Country Club.

Hemingway was assigned a gray ambulance with a large red cross painted on the top. Once a day he navigated hairpin turns on mountainous roads so narrow that the barbed wire that lined each side scratched paint from his Fiat. For three weeks he delivered wounded to distributing stations. Then the war front moved north of Venice. Some ambulance drivers were transferred there, but Hemingway was left behind.

"I'm fed up," he told Brumback one day late in June. "There's nothing here but scenery and too damn much of that. I'm going to get out of this ambulance section and see if I can't find out where the war is."

His quest for action made him volunteer for canteen duty. Behind the lines of trenches and listening posts were emergency canteens where coffee, soup, candy, and cigarettes were given to soldiers taking a break from the front. Hemingway was assigned to Fossalta, a heavily damaged village.

Canteen supplies didn't arrive for a week, and there was little to do, but Hemingway didn't mind. He could hear explosions from the front, and he was glad to be near action. He hung out with Italian soldiers and listened to stories about the war. Although Hemingway quickly picked up pidgin Italian, a young priest usually translated for him in broken English.

When supplies arrived, Hemingway would sometimes bicycle to the trenches and pass out chocolate and cigarettes. On the hot, moonless night of July 8, he carried supplies to Italian soldiers at a forward listening post. The men talked about how loud it was at the front.

Around midnight, Hemingway heard the cough of a big Austrian gun as it sent its projectile toward them. Like others that had rained on the area, it was the size of a five-gallon drum and was packed with scrap metal and steel fragments. Hemingway heard the chug-chug sound as the trench mortar bomb made its way toward them; then he saw the flash of light and felt the intense heat as it exploded. He was thrown down and hit his head hard, temporarily knocking him out. When he regained consciousness he found one soldier dead beside him and heard a nearby soldier crying out in pain. Although his legs felt as if they had been torn apart, and he knew they were bleeding profusely, he stumbled to his feet, hoisted the wounded man over his shoulder and headed for the first aid dugout. After fifty yards, machine gun fire hit him in the leg and he fell. He had no memory of covering the final hundred yards before passing out again, but an Italian officer told him that he had carried the injured soldier to safety.

Other soldiers loaded Hemingway on a stretcher, and for two hours he lay at a dressing station with other soldiers, some dead, some dying, waiting on ambulances. He was transferred to a mobile medical unit where he was given morphine and antitetanus. His friend the priest was administering to the long row of dying and wounded. When he came to Hemingway's stretcher, he murmured holy words and anointed him, just as he had the soldiers.

Doctors took 28 fragments from Hemingway's legs and feet and left some 200 more pieces of metal that were too deep to be removed. From this place he went to a field hospital and lay in a ward for five days awaiting transport. For two days he rode in a train berth, sometimes hearing the clangety-clang of the rails and sometimes hearing only flies buzzing around him as the train sat on a siding, awaiting its turn to move. Four days before his nineteenth birthday, he arrived at the Red Cross hospital in Milan. It was a large stone mansion, and his room on the top floor was high-ceilinged and had a balcony. In contrast to the field hospital, it was a lovely place to recover from his wounds and bask in the knowledge that he would be given an Italian silver medal of valor.

Hemingway wrote to his folks that he was the first American wounded in Italy, even though he knew that in June an ambulance driver had been killed. He described his wounds and two surgeries necessary to remove bullets. He reassured his parents, "There will be no permanent effects from any of the wounds as there are no bones shattered. Even in my knees."

The local newspapers in Oak Park ran articles about Hemingway, and even the letter he had written to his parents appeared in a newspaper. When copies of the newspapers touting his courage reached him in Milan, he wrote to his family, "...I have begun to think, Family, that maybe you didn't appreciate me when I used to reside in the bosom. It's the next best thing to getting killed and reading your own obituary."

As the youngest patient in the hospital, Hemingway enjoyed the fuss and attention paid to him by American nurses. One in particular caught his eye, twenty-six-year-old Agnes von Kurowsky stood out. She flirted with Hemingway, and he responded by falling deeply in love. She reminded him of their seven-year age difference and called him Kid, but he waved away the years as unimportant and called her Mrs. Kid. She was his night nurse, and during the days while she slept, he wrote her long letters.

His recuperation time was spent holding court in his room. He had always been popular with his male friends in a sports-minded-bonding type of way. Now he garnered a sort of hero worship from others. His charismatic personality drew people because of his independent air and his desire to live his life free from societies' traditions. Fellow ambulance drivers came around to visit, other patients went to his room, and even Italian soldiers paid their respects.

Hemingway kept a stash of cognac in his closet to booster his spirits and to serve as a painkiller. When pieces of shrapnel worked their way to the surface, he pried them out using his penknife. He dropped the pieces of metal in a container with the intention of making souvenir rings.

Once he was able to get around on crutches, Hemingway and Agnes planned a trip to the races as a vacation from hospital routine. On that special afternoon, Hemingway refused to leave his room until wound patches had been sewn on his uniform. He didn't want to be thought a loafer on his wonderful afternoon break.

By September he was able to take a holiday with another ambulance driver to a grand hotel on Lake Maggiore. His friend rowed them on the lake, a soothing reminder of Hemingway's days on Walloon Lake in Michigan. In the Italian hotel, Hemingway met an elderly count who played billiards with him and supplied him with champagne. Hemingway enjoyed their enlightening conversations on international affairs and later claimed that the count "brought him up politically."

Upon his return to Milan, Hemingway learned that Agnes was being temporarily transferred to another hospital. He wrote to her daily, sometimes twice a day, and to pass the time while she was away, he managed a week-long trip near the front lines with a couple of other ambulance drivers.

He arrived at the Red Cross headquarters still using a cane. Although he wasn't physically well enough to resume work, he continued to observe all that was around him, paying particular attention to several regiments of Arditi, the fierce Italian soldiers in gray uniforms and black-tasseled caps that cut such swaggering figures. Hemingway was enamored by them, and the fiction was born in his mind that he had not only served with them, but had been wounded while fighting alongside them. That made a much better war story than being wounded while carrying chocolate to some soldiers. Thus, an item was added to what would become the Hemingway Legend, stories of his life that weren't based on facts, but were embellished by the man himself. Some historians claim Hemingway had already fictionalized the account of his wounding. Some feel he rescued no one, but was carried from the scene by stretcher.

The legend grew on its own, too. In late fall, his sister Marcelline attended a movie in Chicago and saw a newsreel about the work of the American Red Cross in Italy. There across the big screen was none other than Ernest Hemingway. He sat in a wheelchair on the porch of the hospital and was being pushed by a pretty nurse. With a big smile, he waved a crutch at the camera. Marcelline called her family, and her parents watched the newsreel the following night.

His sister wrote him about the moment captured on film and wondered if the nurse was the Agnes he had described in his letters. He replied that it wasn't. "Ag is prettier than anybody you guys ever saw. Wait till you see her!"

Hemingway was reunited with Agnes during short periods before he sailed home from Italy in January 1919. They wrote regularly, and he felt confident that she would marry him when she returned to the States.

When his ship docked in New York, Hemingway was met by a reporter from the *Sun*. In an article in the New York newspaper, the reporter claimed that Hemingway's body had more scars than "any other man, in or out of uniform, who defied the shrapnel of the Central Powers."

Hemingway's father and Marcelline greeted him at the train in Chicago. The reunion with other family members at his home cheered him, but Oak

Park was not exciting like Italy. He was lonely for Agnes and his comrades from the Red Cross.

Up in his room on the third floor of his family's home, he secretly drank liqueurs that he'd brought from Italy. Once he offered a drink to Marcelline, and she tasted it but wouldn't swallow. Hemingway urged her to drink. "Don't be afraid to taste all the other things in life that aren't here in Oak Park. This life is all right, but there's a whole big world out there full of people who really feel things. They live and love and die with all their feelings. Taste everything, Sis. Don't be afraid to try new things just because they *are new*. Sometimes I think we only half live over here."

He talked with a reporter from *The Oak Parker* and convinced her that he was a reluctant hero. "I went because I wanted to go," he told her. "I was big and strong, my country needed me, and I went and did whatever I was told—and anything I did outside of that was simply my duty."

The Oak Parker article brought a flood of speaking engagements. Many times Hemingway would take a helmet, the shrapnel-holed pants he'd worn on the night he was wounded, a revolver, and other war memorabilia as visual aids. He talked about the noise, the fear, the smell of war. He wore his military uniform whenever he went out of the house.

The Italian-American community from Chicago and the suburbs gave him two parties to celebrate his contribution to their homeland. They brought food, musical instruments, and red wine to the Hemingway house and sang and celebrated loudly. Hemingway's father allowed only two parties, claiming the noise was a nuisance to the neighbors.

In March came the letter from Agnes. She'd met someone else and broke off with Hemingway. He was so distraught, he developed a fever and took to his bed. Then anger overtook him. He wrote a friend that he hoped that upon Agnes's return to the States she tripped on the dock and broke out all of her front teeth.

As well as writing letters to friends, he wrote short stories using some of his experiences and observations in Italy, but he did not apply for work at a newspaper. Instead, he went north to Michigan, taking a supply of writing materials with him.

SORTING LIFE OUT AFTER THE WAR

Hemingway went to Michigan with his summer friend, Bill Smith, and stayed with Bill's aunt. He helped out with the farm chores that he could manage—spraying apple trees and planting the garden. He still suffered with his war injuries. Pieces of shrapnel worked their way to the surface, and several times he had a local doctor bandage his legs.

But he was well enough to enjoy a fishing trip with Bill. Without his family around, Hemingway openly drank and smoked Russian cigarettes. But he found on his return from the week-long campout that his family had arrived at Windemere Cottage, and his newfound freedom evaporated.

His mother planned to build a cottage for herself across the lake. She couldn't stand the constant noise and confusion of her family and needed occasional breaks from them. The new cottage would provide the solitude she needed and serve as a music studio where she could compose. Hemingway helped with the painting of Grace Cottage, but he didn't approve of it. However, his mother thought that he of all her children should have understood.

"Ernest is very like me," she told Marcelline. "When he gets through this period he's going through, of fighting himself and everybody else, and turns his energy toward something positive, he will be a fine man."

His mother was concerned that Hemingway was not ambitious. She considered him fully healed now, and he was making no effort to find a job at a newspaper, if writing was what he wanted. He laughed when she suggested college. Instead of planning ahead, he did odd jobs around the area and went on long fishing trips with his buddies.

Hemingway had not given up the dream of serious writing. He had several stories he considered publishable, but he needed to learn the business of submitting to magazines. When he discovered that Edwin Balmer, a former *Chicago Tribune* reporter turned novelist, was at the lake for the summer, he arranged to spend an afternoon talking with him.

Balmer gave him the names of editors at several magazines and encouraged Hemingway to submit his work. Hemingway had already sent some stories to *Red Book* and *Saturday Evening Post* and had received rejections. Balmer offered hope, and Hemingway gladly grabbed it.

Hemingway planned more fishing trips with buddies and enjoyed the summer during the times he was away from his family. On one fishing trip in the Upper Peninsula of Michigan, he was getting off the train with all of his gear when he heard the breakman tell the engineer, "Hold her up. There's a cripple and he needs time to get his stuff down."

He had gloried in his war injuries, playing them up for sympathy and adulation, but he had no intention of being a cripple. He wanted admiration, not pity. He was a man, and he intended for no one to forget that. No one should be stronger than he.

With resolve to be a writer, Hemingway stayed at the lake after his family had returned to Oak Park. He visited them briefly in October, but returned to the lake area and rented a room in Petoskey. Each day he wrote on his old typewriter.

In December he spoke to the Ladies' Aid Society at the public library. In the audience was Harriet Connable of Toronto, who was visiting her mother. She was quite impressed with Hemingway and offered him a job as a companion to her son Ralph Jr. while she and her husband wintered in Florida. Ralph Jr. was a year younger than Hemingway and had been lame since birth.

The job was made in heaven for Hemingway. The Connable mansion was huge with a billiard room and a tennis court that had been flooded for winter use as a skating rink. Hemmingway enjoyed both. In the mornings, he pounded away on his typewriter. In the evenings, he accompanied Ralph Jr. to boxing matches, hockey games, plays, or concerts.

Before he left for Florida, Ralph Sr. introduced Hemingway to people at the *Toronto Star*, which had both weekly and daily editions. Determined, Hemingway dropped in at the newspaper office every day until he was given a feature assignment for the *Star Weekly*. One assignment led to another, and he proudly sent copies of his work to his parents.

He still couldn't break into the fiction market. He sent reporter/novelist Balmer several of his stories for suggestions, and Balmer replied that a couple were salable with the caveat that they might not sell immediately. "The funny feature of the writing business is that you simply can not tell what will go; I've seen things in print that I wouldn't believe anyone could possibly buy; and I've seen things turned down that I couldn't see how anyone could pass up."

When Hemingway's job in Toronto ended, he briefly returned to Oak Park, then headed north for another glorious summer in Michigan. But the summer didn't go as he'd planned. His competitive nature surfaced, and he wanted to win at everything. He argued with Bill Smith over finishing a hike first as if it were a contest. He couldn't stand losing in tennis. He had to catch the biggest fish.

He helped little with the cottage, and arguments with his mother became more and more prevalent. She cooked him a 21st birthday supper, but chastised him for being gone on his fishing trips when he was needed at home.

A few days later he was invited on a clandestine midnight picnic which his sisters and neighbors had planned. When the youngsters were discovered returning at three in the morning, Hemingway's mother blamed him because he was older and should know better. The next morning she handed him a letter and told him to leave. In her letter she had written that he should stop loafing, stop using people, and stop spending money lavishly. When he matured and changed his ways, he would be welcomed back.

Hemingway was hurt and told friends that he was now homeless. But that didn't stop him from going on another fishing trip. When it was over, he hitched a ride with Bill to Chicago. Hemingway planned to stay with Y. K. Smith, Bill's brother, while he looked for a job.

Fortune smiled on Hemingway. While staying at Y. K.'s place, he met many writers including Sherwood Anderson, author of *Winesburg, Ohio*, who enjoyed giving advice on writing. He also met 28-year-old Elizabeth Hadley Richardson of St. Louis. In describing the moment he saw her, he later said to his brother Leicester, "an intense feeling came over me. I knew she was the girl I was going to marry." They were together constantly during her three-week visit at Y. K.'s and wrote of love after she went back home.

His affections softened toward his family, and he began healing the rift. When he finally landed a job for $40 a week writing for *The Cooperative Commonwealth*, he wrote his mother the details of his job. "Am being frightfully good in pursuit of your instructions. At least you told me to be good didn't you? Being so anyway. Very busy, very good, and very tired."

With a bit of extra cash, Hemingway managed to make it to St. Louis to see Hadley. Two weeks later she and some friends traveled to Chicago. She introduced her friend Ruth Bradfield to Hemingway. Ruth was awed by Hadley's beau.

> He was slender and moved well. His face had the symmetry of fine bony structure and he had a small elastic mouth that stretched from ear to ear when he laughed. He laughed aloud a lot from quick humor.... His focused attention to the person he was talking with was immensely flattering.... He generated excitement because he was so intense about everything, about writing and boxing, about good food and drink. Everything we did took on new importance when he was with us.

The wedding was set for September 3, 1921, in Michigan with the honeymoon at Windemere Cottage. For a short time, Hemingway got cold feet when he thought of all the freedom he was losing, of all the streams he loved to fish he wouldn't see again, and of all his bachelor friends he was giving up. But he loved Hadley and the wedding took place.

For a short while the couple rented a small apartment and lived on Hadley's trust fund, somewhere around $3000 a year. With this guaranteed income and a new job as the European correspondent for the *Toronto Star Daily*, Hemingway was ready to continue his education in writing. The newlyweds were headed to Paris.

CREATING THE IMAGE

During his first year in Paris, Ernest Hemingway learned the craft of writing. He honed his natural talent by analyzing works of his fellow expatriates. He disdained the talk and rhetoric of writing in favor of those who were actually writing: Gertrude Stein, Ezra Pound, John Dos Passos, and Irish novelist James Joyce.

Hemingway learned discipline in writing. Besides adhering to deadlines for the *Toronto Star*, he learned to stop a short story at a spot where he knew what would happen next. When he picked up his pen the next day, he could edit what he'd written the day before and immediately start writing where he'd left off. He didn't think about his short stories when he wasn't writing. Instead he observed life around him and made notes. He believed his subconscious would work on the story.

He wanted to write "one true sentence"—a straight direct sentence that showed emotions. He later explained, "If I started to write elaborately, or like someone introducing or presenting something, I found that I could cut that scrollwork or ornament out and throw it away and start with the first true simple declarative sentence I had written."

In February of 1923, after Hadley had told Hemingway that she was pregnant, they traveled to Rapallo, Italy, to escape the chilling dampness of Paris. Hemingway wrote little vignettes in their hotel room during the day, but at night he and Hadley went out for dinner and drinks. At one restaurant they met Robert McAlmon, an American poet and short story writer who had married a British heiress and begun a career as a publisher of Contact Editions.

McAlmon later wrote that his feelings about Hemingway were mixed because of Hemingway's odd behavior. "At times he was deliberately hard-boiled and case-hardened." But McAlmon saw a different side, too.

> Again he appeared deliberately innocent, sentimental, the hurt, soft, but fairly sensitive boy trying to conceal hurt, wanting to be brave, not bitter or cynical but being somewhat both, and somehow on the defensive, suspicions lurking in his peering analytic glances at a person with whom he was talking. He approached a café with a small-boy, tough-guy swagger, and before strangers of whom he was doubtful, a potential snarl of scorn played on his large-lipped, rather loose mouth.

Hadley said Hemingway "was then the kind of man to whom men, women, children, and dogs were attracted. It was something." That something must have impressed McAlmon, who was generous to Hemingway. Back in Paris that spring, he mentioned he was going to Spain and upon learning that Hemingway yearned to go, he offered to help with expenses. Newsman and new publisher Bill Bird joined the twosome in Spain.

Hemingway had felt the call to Spain for some time. Gertrude Stein had told him of wonderful bullfights, and he wanted to see them firsthand. He was not disappointed. The drama of the bullring fascinated him. It was a struggle for life and death, although death always won—always for the bull, but sometimes for the matador. The crowd, the noise, the horses that could be gored until their entrails hung out, the swords, the dedication of the bull, the dance of the matadors—all made indelible impressions on an impressionable young man.

The ritual killing of the bull, the art of sticking the sword in the exact spot to instantly take its life, took on tragic significance in his mind. On his days in Spain, he scribbled notes: "In the first place, not going apologize for bull fighting. Is a tragedy—not a sport. Have only seen 16—hope to see 300 more before I die. Only thing that brings man opposit[e]s of life and death."

The trip with McAlmon resulted in an offer of a first book with Contact Editions. Although Hemingway was already scheduled to write for Bill Bird's Three Mountains Press, he immediately agreed to give McAlmon the stories he had—all three of them and some poems. That left nothing for Bird's book, but Hemingway set to work on more vignettes that would work for that volume.

He was writing about the bullfights, but he wanted to experience more. In July he and Hadley set out for Pamplona and the week-long Fiesta of San Fermin. The music, the dancing, the young men running down the street in front of the bulls as they charged toward the bullring—all became vivid memories in the writer's mind. Hemingway wrote five vignettes from his observations of bullfighting's pageantry.

Early in August, Hemingway saw the proofs of his first book, *Three Stories and Ten Poems*. It was quite a thin little booklet, and he suggested to McAlmon that some blank pages be added at the beginning and end to fatten it. On August 13, the first copies had been bound. Hemingway and Hadley stood outside Sylvia Beach's bookstore staring at the copies displayed in the window. Then they went inside and got the author's four free copies that were charged to McAlmon.

On August 26, Hadley and Hemingway set sail for Canada. Earlier, Hemingway had told the *Toronto Star* editor that he would return in the fall for a regular job on the newspaper. His intention was to earn enough money to return to Paris in a year. Hadley was for the move, since she did not want to have their baby in Europe.

The move started off well enough, but quickly soured. Hemingway's new boss disliked him and sent him on inconsequential out-of-town assignments. He was on a return trip to Toronto when his son, John (nicknamed Bumby), was born, and he was furious that he had not been with Hadley.

He worked hard. He worked late. And he had no time for his own writing, barely finding time to send a review copy of his first book to a critic. He missed Paris. He was 24 years old, and he felt that every month in Toronto took years off his literary career. His book of vignettes, *in our time*, would be out soon, and he wanted desperately to write seriously. He wanted out of journalism.

Hadley wrote a friend, "Our hearts are heavy, heavy, just when we ought to be so happy."

As soon as Hadley was strong and the baby was old enough to travel, Hemingway quit his job and his little family sailed for Paris. With a new apartment in a better neighborhood, although next to a noisy sawmill, Hemingway was able to write, but not at home. With the baby's cries and the sawmill's whine, he found that writing in cafés was much more to his liking.

When *in our time* came out, his parents ordered several copies of it. But after reading one vignette where a man contracted gonorrhea, his father sent the books back to the publisher. He told his family that he didn't want such filth in his house, and he was ashamed that his son had fallen away from his Christian upbringing.

When Hemingway learned the books had been returned, he bitterly resented it and maligned life in Oak Park in a letter to his parents. "I wonder what was the matter, whether the pictures were too accurate and the attitude toward life not sufficiently distorted to please who ever bought the books or what?"

Hemingway made no money from his first two books. He expected none. His goal was to have his work published and have it noticed by critics. He believed with hard work and a little luck the payoff would come later, and it would be through the New York publishing world.

Through Ezra Pound's influence, Hemingway was given a job as sub-editor on Ford Maddox Ford's new literary magazine, *Transatlantic Review*. Hemingway's two books were reviewed in the magazine, and Ford also accepted several of his short stories. Ford later recalled, "I did not read more than six words of his before I decided to publish everything that he sent me."

Hemingway didn't care for Ford, but he learned from him. Ford had mastered the art of self-promotion, and Hemingway took note of how it was done. Through Ford he met writer Harold Loeb. He and Loeb played tennis together, although Hemingway's war knee injury made him move slowly on the court.

Hemingway delighted in Paris. His writing was flowing, and he produced several short stories and still had time for fun. He sometimes earned a few francs by sparring with professional boxers at a gym and told a friend that the money was for his return-to-Spain fund. He continued his friendships with other writers, still gleaning what he could from their expertise.

July again found the Hemingways in Pamplona. Hemingway's enthusiasm for bullfighting was contagious, and he'd convinced several friends to meet them for the fiesta. Dos Passos, McAlmon, Bill Bird and his wife, a former friend from WWI, and Donald Ogden Stewart, another expatriate writer, joined the fun. Stewart even joined Hemingway in the ring when the young bulls with padded horns were let loose for amateur matadors. Stewart was tossed in the air by a bull and cracked two ribs. He later admitted he'd entered the ring only to prove his bravery to Hemingway, who had a way of infecting others with his passions.

On his return to Paris, Hemingway completed another story and sent others out to American magazines, but rejections came back. The *Transatlantic Review*, which had published several of his stories, was in great financial trouble and about to fold. But Hemingway still held out hope for his own writing. His new idea was to put the short stories in one book interspersed with the vignettes from *in our time*. The new volume would be called *In Our Time*, with proper capital letters. When Dos Passos traveled to New York, he took Hemingway's manuscripts with him and called on Don Stewart, and together they decided which editors to approach about the book.

While awaiting news from New York, the Hemingways sublet their apartment and set off for Schruns, Austria, for a skiing holiday. The place was cheap. Even with a fulltime nurse for the baby, it was cheaper to live there than in Paris. Hemingway tried to write, but several attempts resulted in uncompleted manuscripts, so he spent his time writing letters, hiking, and skiing.

At Christmas he heard from Stewart that his book of stories had been rejected by a publisher because it contained too much sex. If it had been in a novel, he could have gotten by with it. Upbeat, Stewart wrote that he had a couple of other publishers in mind; one was Sherwood Anderson's and Harold Loeb's publisher, Boni & Liveright.

In February 1925, cables from Stewart and Loeb arrived at Schruns. Liveright was going to publish the work. When Liveright's offer of $200 advance came via telegram, Hemingway wired back, "DELIGHTED ACCEPT."

The Hemingways returned to Paris and celebrated with Loeb and his girlfriend. Also at Loeb's apartment were two sisters, Pauline and Virginia

Pfeiffer, from a wealthy Arkansas family. Pauline worked for Paris *Vogue* as a writer and model, and she and Hemingway carried on an animated conversation.

Also upon his return, Hemingway found in his mail a letter from Max Perkins, an editor at Scribner's. He had read *in our time* and wondered if Hemingway had a bigger project that he could consider. Hemingway didn't, and his contract with Liveright gave the publisher an option on his next two books.

How had Perkins heard of Hemingway? F. Scott Fitzgerald, who was published by Scribner's, had read *in our time* and recommended it to the editor. It wasn't long before the two writers met in a Paris bar. They were both products of the American Midwest, had dominating mothers, couldn't live up to the expectations of their fathers, and both wanted to make a mark on the literary scene. Throughout May and June, they were together often, talking writing. Fitzgerald's *The Great Gatsby* had come out, and he was disappointed in the sales figures. But, he advised Hemingway, short story sales were even worse unless a writer had built a name with a novel.

Hemingway knew he'd have to try a novel, but how was it done? He had started the one in Chicago that Gertrude Stein had said to start over. Well, he had to—that first one had been stolen at the train station. He mulled it over as he made plans for his annual pilgrimage to Pamplona.

The crew this time included Hadley, his old friend Bill Smith from Michigan days, Don Stewart, Harold Loeb, and two new acquaintances— Duff Twysden, a liberated Englishwoman with quite a capacity for drink and laughter, and her lover, Pat Guthrie.

From the beginning, things didn't go well. Loeb and Duff had earlier spent a week together, and he was quite smitten with her, although she'd told him it was over between them. Hemingway had a crush on Duff, although they never had an affair. With constant drinking, little sleep, and tension between them, it was no wonder that tempers flared. Hemingway taunted Loeb, asked him to leave, and nearly came to a fist fight with him.

Stewart remembered Hemingway's viciousness quite well.

> The mean streak was a booby trap kind of thing. There's no explaining it…. He wasn't mean; he was charismatic; and it was for this very reason that the mean streak startled you so when it came to the surface….He didn't have to have a reason to be mean. It was more of a mood thing.

After the blowup, Hemingway apologized to Loeb. Then the fiesta of 1925 was over, and it was time to move on. Hadley and Hemingway traveled in Spain, and he began writing a story with barely disguised characters from that week in Pamplona. The story grew to novel length. He wrote all during the holiday in Spain and finished the first draft of *The Sun Also Rises* in Paris, less than two months after he'd begun.

This book was good. He knew it was good. He started revising the book and plotting its publication.

When *In Our Time* came out in October, it was well received by American critics. *Time* magazine said, "Make no mistake, Ernest Hemingway is somebody; a new, honest, un-'literary' transcriber of life—a Writer."

His work was compared to his friend Sherwood Anderson's writing, and Hemingway didn't like that. His work was compared to the modernists, including Gertrude Stein. Hemingway didn't like that, either, and he turned against his old friends.

He didn't want his Pamplona book to be published by Liveright. That was Loeb's publisher and Anderson's publisher. Hemingway wanted Fitzgerald's publisher, Scribner's, and he wanted to be bigger than Fitzgerald. His competitive spirit reared its very strong head.

To break the contract with Liveright, he had to present a manuscript that Liveright would reject. Then he'd be free to take his good book to Scribner's. In ten days he dashed off *The Torrents of Spring* and sent it to Liveright. The book was a parody of Anderson's latest novel. Since Anderson was Liveright's best-selling author, of course the publisher wouldn't accept the satire.

Hadley pleaded with Hemingway not to send the book; Anderson had been so kind to them. But Hemingway was adamant. This was one of many times that Hemingway nourished a friendship and then broke it off when there was nothing more to be gained by the friendship. As Fitzgerald said, Hemingway would "always give a helping hand to a man on a ledge a little higher up."

Pauline Pfeiffer encouraged Hemingway to send the Anderson parody. Pauline had become a good friend of Hadley's. She visited the Hemingways on many occasions, and after Hadley would retire for the night, Hemingway would walk Pauline to the corner to hail a taxi. On one of those late nights, the two confessed their love to each other. But Hemingway also still loved Hadley.

In December the Hemingways returned to their winter haunt of Schruns, Austria. On Christmas Day of 1925, Pauline arrived to spend a couple of weeks. Hemingway wrote that nothing was ever the same after that.

When Liveright rejected Hemingway's parody, he rejoiced and left Hadley in Schruns, Pauline in Paris, and he set off for New York to see Max Perkins. He wrote Hadley the good news that Perkins had offered him $1,500 advance for both *The Torrents of Spring* and *The Sun Also Rises* plus a royalty.

Hemingway returned to Paris and stayed a few days with Pauline before catching the train to Schruns. It was April before Hadley discovered the affair. A separation followed and then the divorce, which was final in January 1927.

Hadley was crushed by Hemingway's betrayal, but she was not bitter. She never believed that Pauline's money had anything to do with the affair. "Pauline fell madly in love with him. And Ernest was weak in the sense that if someone wanted him very much, he was tremendously touched by it."

Hemingway never forgave himself for betraying Hadley. Although he loved Pauline, the delicate balance between his joyous side and his depressed side tipped a bit toward the dark side.

He claimed to have been baptized by a priest during the war when he was wounded and was therefore a Catholic, as Pauline was. Since he and Hadley weren't married in the Catholic faith, his marriage to her was declared invalid. Hemingway married Pauline on May 10, 1927, by a priest in a Catholic church.

A PLACE TO COME BACK TO

The Torrents of Spring, the parody of Sherwood Anderson's book, did not sell very well. In his typical style, Hemingway shrugged off the thought that he had hurt a friend. When he saw Anderson in Paris, he thought they'd had a fine time, but Anderson remembered the event differently and said Hemingway's "absorption in his ideas" had "affected his capacity for friendship."

The Sun Also Rises was doing very well. The public was buying the book and talking about it. Hemingway's mother read it and called it "one of the filthiest books of the year." Hemingway was angry at first, but since he cared little what his mother thought, he took this as her usual nastiness toward him. In a magnanimous gesture, he'd assigned the book's royalties to Hadley as a divorce settlement.

Men Without Women, a collection of short stories he'd written during the turbulent time between his separation from Hadley and his marriage to Pauline, was well-received when it appeared from Scribner's in October 1927.

Hemingway was gaining favor with the public and felt he was at a good place in his writing career when a string of accidents occurred. He was carrying his son when Bumby threw his hand up to Hemingway's face. The boy's fingernail cut Hemingway's pupil, and for several days Hemingway's vision was a blur. This episode made him fearful of one day losing his sight.

A few months later in his own bathroom, Hemingway mistakenly pulled on the skylight chain instead of the toilet chain. The ancient skylight crashed down on his head, cutting a gash that required nine stitches.

The scar was still purple when he and Pauline left Paris in the spring of 1928 and sailed for America. She was pregnant and did not want to have her baby in Europe. The plan was to disembark at Key West, Florida, a nine-square-mile island at the tip of the Florida Keys. Pauline's rich Uncle Gus had bought them a car which they would pick up there.

Shipment of the car was delayed, which allowed Hemingway time to enjoy fishing in the coastal waters. Just as he loved to fish for trout in his early Michigan days, now he delighted in fishing for tarpon. Before the trip, he had begun a new novel about the World War, and he spent mornings working on it and afternoons fishing or making friends at a local bar, where he drank bootlegged liquor from Cuba. Although Prohibition was still the law, in Key West the residents adhered to a live-and-let-live philosophy. It was the exact atmosphere Hemingway was looking for.

At 28 years old, Hemingway was well on his way to establishing his legend. He walked to his favorite bar in old moccasins, a rope for a belt to hold up canvas shorts, and fish stains on a worn-out T-shirt. He looked like a seedy character, but he didn't care. He was surrounded by people he liked and who liked him. He impressed his new friends with tales of his war wound in Italy, the bull fights in Spain, skiing and hiking in Switzerland, and the cafés in Paris. With all of these experiences, he seemed worldly-wise, and his new friends called him Papa.

Pauline was ready to forsake the heat of Florida for her parents' home in Arkansas, but Hemingway wanted to stay and fish. Finally, she went ahead via train, while Hemingway invited friends down for a fishing expedition.

The assembled group, mostly Paris expatriates who like Hemingway had returned to the United States, was known as the Mob. Swimming, fishing, eating, and hard drinking took up much of Hemingway's time, but he still allotted early morning for work on his novel.

At the end of May, he drove to Piggott, Arkansas, where he picked up Pauline and took her to Kansas City to have the baby. After baby Patrick was born on June 28, 1928, and as soon as mother and son were able to travel, the Hemingways returned to Arkansas via train. Hemingway continued to work on his manuscript, but Piggott had nothing to offer for entertainment except trap shooting. He was bored there, and he escaped as soon as he could. He picked up the car in Kansas City and headed to Wyoming. At a dude ranch, he continued his schedule of writing on the book in the mornings and fishing cold mountain streams in the afternoon. But he missed Spain. This was the first time he'd missed the running of the bulls in Pamplona in five years.

Pauline joined him in August, and by the end of the month he'd finished the rough draft of *A Farewell to Arms*. By the end of September they returned to Arkansas to check on the baby, but Hemingway found he was no fonder of the place than he'd been earlier. He and his wife left again. During a stop in Chicago, Hemingway was struck by how old and ill his father looked. Later in New York he watched boxing matches and talked to Perkins about the new book. He and Pauline visited the Fitzgeralds in Delaware, but Scott Fitzgerald was drunk and after one night the Hemingways left convinced that Fitzgerald was self-destructing.

Key West was a welcomed sight after their travels, but Hemingway had barely unpacked his wife and baby at the rental house when he journeyed on the train to New York to fetch his son Bumby. Hadley had put the five-year-old on a ship, and he had crossed the Atlantic in the care of a steward.

Hemingway and his oldest son were in a train station when he received a wire from his sister in Oak Park. His father had died that morning. Hemingway put Bumby in the care of a porter and sent him on his way to Florida, but he was short of cash for the trip to Illinois. He wired Fitzgerald, who immediately sent money.

In Oak Park, Hemingway learned the tragic story of his father's death. Burdened with financial problems and facing health problems from diabetes, the older Hemingway chose to end his life rather than face possible amputation of a foot. He had burned some personal papers in the basement furnace, climbed the stairs to his bedroom, and shot himself with his father's revolver.

Hemingway wrote a short note to Fitzgerald. "You were damned good and also bloody effective to get me that money…. My Father shot himself as I suppose you may have read in the papers … I was fond as hell of my father and feel too punk—also sick etc.—to write a letter but wanted to thank you."

After the funeral, Hemingway returned to Key West, where he blocked the recent family tragedy from his mind and worked six hours a day on revisions of *A Farewell to Arms*, which would be serialized in *Scribner's Magazine* before coming out in book form. As the dutiful son, he wrote his mother that he could help her out financially as long as he had money and could borrow it when he didn't. He also wanted Marcelline and her husband to contribute to the household because "they are rich and have always been very great friends of the family while I live by my pen and have been more or less of an outcast."

With the revisions of his book completed, Hemingway celebrated in his usual style with friends descending on Key West for fishing expeditions. Even Max Perkins came down to collect the manuscript and cram as many hours of fishing into a day as possible.

Before long, it was time for Paris again. Hemingway packed up his family and installed them in an apartment. He returned Bumby to Hadley and visited with friends, but few old friends remained, as he had a habit of using them up and discarding them after a few years.

Hemingway and Pauline set off for the 1929 fiesta in Pamplona. He was unable to write as they traveled around Spain following the bullfight circuit. Instead of stories, he wrote letters, which was his habit when his creative juices weren't flowing. Fitzgerald was in Europe and was having trouble finishing a book. Hemingway wrote an encouraging letter and said that the depression Fitzgerald was experiencing was known to all writers. "Summer's a discouraging time to work—You dont [sic] feel death coming on the way it does in the fall when the boys really put pen to paper."

The Hemingways were back in Paris when they received splendid reviews of *A Farewell to Arms* and learned from Perkins' cables that sales were going well. Even after the stock market crash, book sales continued. A rather inaccurate, but flattering, profile of Hemingway had been published in *The New Yorker* magazine. And Hemingway's reputation as Writer grew.

Hemingway was getting homesick for Key West, so after a trip to Switzerland, his family sailed home. By March, many of the Mob had returned to Key West for winter sunshine.

Hemingway planned a trip to Dry Tortugas, an island 65 miles west of Key West. The Mob, including editor Max Perkins, packed plenty of supplies for the week-long excursion. The group fished, drank, and swapped stories, with Hemingway leading the way. A fierce tropical storm marooned them for seventeen days, and they were reduced to eating only fish by the time they could leave the island. Perkins called the vacation "a grand adventure" and said, "This town is certainly good for Ernest."

Hemingway loved the town, but he was never tied down to one spot for long. He was already planning a safari for Africa, financed by Pauline's Uncle Gus, but he was now ready to go West.

At a ranch in Wyoming, Hemingway settled down to work on a project near to his heart—bullfighting. He had written an article on bullfighting for *Fortune* magazine, and now he intended to make it a book-length project. As was his habit, he worked on the manuscript in the mornings and in the afternoons fished or rode a horse. Evenings he talked with the other guests, but usually ended up at the bunkhouse talking to the hands. They thought he was a wonderful guy and called him 'Pop.'

After a neighboring rancher complained about a bear killing his cattle, a ranch hand took Hemingway to the high country to set a bear trap. They killed a big horse out in the sun so it would ripen and the bear would smell it. Later when they went to check on it, Hemingway had another of his accidents. His horse bolted, carrying him into a thick woods, and he suffered cuts on his arms and legs and a very deep one on his chin. In need of stitches, Hemingway was taken to Cody to the nearest doctor. The tightness of the stitches pulled his lips to one side, and he said he looked like he was growling, "the hell you say." But the next day, he rode out to the bear trap and successfully killed the bear with one shot.

On the way back from a hunting trip in Montana, Hemingway met with a much more serious accident. He was driving the car when he was blinded by headlights and ended upside down in a ditch. Hemingway's passengers escaped harm, but his arm was broken in a unique spiral fracture above the elbow. After surgery, Hemingway had to remain flat in bed for nearly a month. Seven weeks after the accident, he was allowed to leave the hospital.

Through the spring in Key West, Hemingway nursed his arm, writing only letters, but able to fish some with his left hand. When it was obvious that Pauline was pregnant again, he made plans to go to Europe for the summer, return to have the baby in Kansas City, and then winter in Key West in a place of their own. They looked for a suitable place and found an old stone house with balconies at 907 Whitehead Street. Pauline's Uncle Gus bought the house for them. It was badly in need of renovation, but the Hemingways would deal with that when they returned from abroad.

In May they arrived in Paris, and Hemingway spent the summer in Spain researching his bullfighting book. Many of his entries in his glossary of bullfighting terms for *Death in the Afternoon* turned into mini-essays. He still lacked two chapters when the Hemingways returned to the States. They sent Patrick to Arkansas with his new French nanny and traveled to Kansas City. Here Hemingway revised his manuscript until Pauline had a baby boy, named Gregory.

Chaos reigned at their new 80-year-old house in Key West, but the Hemingways settled in among boxes, carpenters, and plumbers. The leaky roof was repaired, the house was rewired, and new water pipes were hooked to a huge cistern for catching rain water since there was no city water in Key West.

Behind the house stood a two-story outbuilding that was at one time a carriage house with servants' quarter above. This was Hemingway's writing area, and he initially furnished it with a wood-frame chair with leather bottom and back pieces and a round table. Boxes of manuscripts lined the walls. It was as Pauline described, a "lightly organized wastepaper can." But here he was able to finish the revisions of *Death in the Afternoon* and immediately start on short stories, which would be published in the book *Winner Take Nothing*.

He relaxed from writing with his fishing expeditions to Dry Tortugas and plans for the African safari. But it was a horrible year of the Depression, and since Uncle Gus was footing the bill for the safari and his stocks were down, the trip was postponed another year. Instead, Hemingway went with Key West friends to Cuba to fish for marlin. The two-week trip stretched to over two months as Hemingway was delighted with Havana's nightlife and the sport of marlin fishing.

In the summer, the Hemingways left their boys with a nanny in Arkansas and drove out to Wyoming. Pauline stayed only a couple of months since she felt the baby might need her. Hemingway fished and hunted and worked on more short stories.

Once back in Key West for the winter, Hemmingway's creative juices continued to flow, and he sold some stories to *Scribner's Magazine* and began working on articles for the new *Esquire* magazine. He had started a long story set in Key West, Cuba, and the Gulf Stream. Of course, research for this story demanded that Hemingway spend a couple months in Cuba fishing for marlin.

In August 1933, Pauline and Hemingway left their boys in the care of servants and Hemingway's sister in Key West, and they sailed for Europe. Their first stop was Spain where they took in the bullfights. They spent the fall in Paris, and finally the trip to Africa. A friend from Key West, Charles Thompson, joined them for the safari.

From the beginning, the safari was a hunting contest. The first lion was supposed to be reserved for Pauline. She wounded it, but Hemingway then killed it. The native members of the expedition lifted Pauline to their shoulders and carried her into camp in celebration. Hemingway fumed that they all knew he had shot the lion and the whole thing was a bad lie.

Although it was not spoken aloud, the big competition was between Hemingway and the easy-going Thompson. By the final leg of the safari, Thompson had regularly shot bigger game. When they found kudu, Thompson's first kill seemed small. Hemingway set out to beat it, and he did. But when he returned to camp with two sets of huge kudu horns, he saw that Thompson's latest kill was even bigger. Hemingway wrestled with envy all through the night, and by morning he had made peace with it, but he vowed to return to Africa for another round.

From Africa the Hemingways went to Europe, then sailed for New York, where Hemingway ordered a custom-built 38-foot power yacht. In April 1934, Hemingway and Pauline headed to Key West for a reunion with their boys. They had been gone nearly eight months.

Hemingway immediately began writing the story of the African trip. But when his boat, the *Pilar*, was delivered, writing alternated with fishing expeditions. By the end of the year he'd finished the book and sold first serial rights to *Scribner's Magazine*.

The following spring of 1935, Hemingway set out for a new adventure on the island of Bimini and met with another bizarre accident. While fishing one day, he hooked a shark and prepared to gaff it with his left hand and shoot it with his right. Somehow the bullets ricocheted, and Hemingway shot himself through the calves of both legs.

Once on the island, he boxed with local challengers, drank heavily and fished for tuna. His activities left little time for writing. Upon his return to Key West, Hemingway complained that guests kept him from writing, but he slowly got back to work with more magazine articles and stories. He had earlier finished the long story set in Key West in the Depression, and he started another featuring the same character, Harry Morgan. When it was finished, he started another and considered combining the stories into one book, *To Have and Have Not*.

While on Bimini during the summer of 1936, Hemingway met another Scribner's novelist, Marjorie Rawlings. She tried to make sense of the man she'd seen gentle while sober and while drunk using a hanging tuna for a punching bag. She thought he must suffer an "inner conflict between the sporting life and the literary life; between sporting people and the artist."

He explained his life to her in a letter.

> As for being Sportsman being Artist. I always fished and shot since I could carry a canepole or a single-barrelled shotgun; not to show off but for great inner pleasure and almost complete satisfaction. Have not been writing as long but get the same pleasure, and you do it alone, only it is a goddamned sight harder to do and if I did nothing else (no fish, no shoot, no drink) would probably go nuts doing it with the difficulty, the times in between when you can't do it, the always being short of what you want to do, the rest of it with all of which you have probably lived some time and various places.

REPORTING THE WARS

He knew he should be in Spain, Hemingway wrote to a friend, but instead of heading to the country that was embroiled in a civil war in 1936, he went to Wyoming for the summer. He was putting the Harry Morgan stories together as a novel. In the fall, his conscience bothered him, and he felt he should go, but the book wasn't finished.

Around Thanksgiving, the North America Newspaper Alliance offered Hemingway a job as a foreign correspondent. Now he had a reason for going to Spain. His hope was to raise the consciousness of Americans and get support for the Spanish Republic. Still the book was unfinished, so he delayed a while longer.

One December day, Hemingway was in his favorite bar in Key West when in walked a lovely young blonde. Journalist and successful novelist Martha Gellhorn was on vacation with her mother and brother. Hemingway was immediately attracted to her, and they talked long hours about the Spanish Civil War.

Even after her family had departed, Martha stayed in Key West and hung around with Hemingway. She wrote her friend First Lady Eleanor Roosevelt that she was seeing Hemingway and called him "an odd bird, very lovable and full of fire and a marvelous storyteller. (In a writer this is imagination, in anyone else it's lying. That's where the genius comes in.)"

Once she left, Hemingway made an excuse for a quick trip to New York and hooked up with Martha in Miami. Again talk turned to going to Spain.

Hemingway had told Perkins that his book was finished, but he had lots of revising to do, so he promised the finished version of *To Have and To Have Not* by June. Spain called, and his ship departed near the end of February. By mid-March Martha Gellhorn was on her way. They met in Madrid, and their affair began in earnest. Hemingway sent regular dispatches to the newspaper service, and Martha sent articles to *Collier's*.

While Hemingway was gone, Pauline had a swimming pool built in the backyard as a surprise. Built with her own money, it was then the only pool south of Miami. Her hope was that Hemingway would relax beside it and be content when he returned from Spain.

But he was cantankerous when he returned in May and complained that the pool had cost him his last cent and had a penny symbolically stamped near the edge of the pool. He worked on his book and was in and out of Key West, speaking at a writers' congress, narrating a Spanish Republic propaganda film, and showing the film to the President and Mrs. Roosevelt. On each trip he saw Martha.

Hemingway was on his way back to Spain in August. Martha joined him there, and he began work on a play, *The Fifth Column*, closely based on his wartime activities and his relationship with her.

By now Pauline knew that her marriage was in jeopardy. She sailed for Paris in December and awaited a visa for Spain. It never came, but Hemingway went to her. Their reunion did not go well, but they returned home together, and for a while they pretended that nothing was wrong. Hemingway fished off the shores of Cuba and tried to write, but couldn't. He was a bully to everyone around him, and he wrote Perkins that he was in a gigantic jam, one that he mostly had made himself.

He headed back to Europe in March 1938. There, he continued to write news copy and made many trips to the front. Once he and other correspondents came up behind a truckload of singing Spaniards. Moments later on a sharp curve Hemingway witnessed the truck careening off the road. He leaped from his car and was down on his knees among the injured and dying, applying bandages, and offering comfort. Martha later commented that she thought the war years were "the only time in his life when he was not the most important thing there was. He really cared about the Republic and he cared about that war."

Back in Key West in June, he tried to get along with Pauline, and still he was restless. He drove the family to Wyoming and worked on a preface for an anthology that would include his play and 49 stories. With it finished in August, he sailed back to Paris to meet Martha. He entered a turbulent Spain once more in November, realized the destruction of the Spanish Republic was imminent, and left for the States.

He'd made four trips to Spain during the war, and he had plenty of new experiences to write about. He explained to a friend about his work, "But what I have to do now is write. As long as there is a war you always think perhaps you will be killed so you have nothing to worry about. But now I am not killed so I have to work. ... living is much more difficult and complicated than dying and it is just as hard as ever to write."

His domestic situation showed little improvement, but he remedied that by going to Cuba and returning to Key West only when necessary. He had begun a novel set during the Spanish Civil War and was obsessed by it.

When Martha joined him in April 1939, she found him contentedly writing away in a dirty little hotel room. Unhappy with the surroundings, she scouted the area around Havana and found a dilapidated old estate near the village of San Francisco de Paula. Hemingway thought the Finca Vigia unfit, but Martha saw possibilities. It was a one-story house on top of a hill with a view of the sea and of Havana. A 60-foot living room made it perfect for entertaining. On the 15 acres were an old tennis court overgrown with weeds and a swimming pool with brackish water, but both could be reclaimed.

While Hemingway was away on a fishing trip, she rented the Finca and hired a painter to whitewash it, a couple of gardeners to tame the grounds, a carpenter to build some furniture, and a cook. When he returned, Hemingway approved, and before his 40th birthday he and Martha had moved in. They shared the monthly expenses, with Hemingway responsible for his own liquor costs.

In August he drove Martha to St. Louis to visit her mother and continued alone to Wyoming, where his three sons were to join him. He arrived at the ranch on the day war broke out in Europe, September 1, 1939, and stayed up most of the night listening to news on the radio.

Pauline made a brief visit to the ranch, but it was obvious that all was over between husband and wife. Hemingway sent Pauline and the boys away and called Martha to meet him in Sun Valley, Idaho, a new resort that had asked him to come visit as a celebrity draw. Martha stayed until she was called by *Collier's* to go to Finland as a correspondent.

Hemingway continued work on the war novel, *For Whom the Bell Tolls*, but he was not pleased to be alone in the evenings. In December he returned to Key West to find it empty. Pauline and the boys were spending Christmas in New York. He loaded all his belongings and left the Key West house for good. Now the Finca was his home.

When Martha returned from Europe in January, he was hard at work on the novel. His routine was simple. He wrote in the morning and had a drink before lunch at two. During siesta time, he read. Later he played tennis, then had a few drinks with friends. Once a week he went to the Floridita bar in Havana to talk and drink. Other times he shot live pigeons at a club, and he bought some roosters and joined a cockfighting club.

He wrote to his publisher, Charles Scribner:

> I have to write to be happy whether I get paid for it or not. But it is a hell of a disease to be born with. I like to do it. Which is even worse. That makes it from a disease into a vice. Then I want to do it better than anybody has ever done it which makes it into an obsession. An obsession is terrible.

Hemingway finished *For Whom the Bell Tolls* in July and had revised it and was reading proofsheets in Sun Valley, Idaho, in September. He knew this book was good, and he had big hopes that it would bring him much more than the $6,000 he had made in 1939.

His hopes were justified. Scribner's printed a huge number of books and contracted for the Book of the Month club edition. In addition, Hemingway sold the movie rights to Paramount Pictures for $100,000, the highest price paid for film rights up to that time.

Hemingway's divorce from Pauline was announced publicly on November 4, 1940, and 17 days later he married Martha. As a Christmas present to himself and Martha, he bought the Finca.

Things were going very well when he heard from Perkins that Scott Fitzgerald had died from a heart attack at the age of 44. The two writers had had an on-again, off-again type of relationship, but they had turned to each other during difficult times. Hemingway had recently sent Fitzgerald a copy of his new book and received a reply congratulating him on its financial success and stating that no one could write a better novel. "I envy you like hell and there is no irony in this. I envy you the time it will give you to do what you want."

The money gave Hemingway security that he hadn't had before, although it didn't let him do exactly what he wanted. When Martha went to China on assignment from *Collier's*, he went with her, but as an unwilling companion. When she voiced her frustration with the poor, dirty conditions in the country, he repeated time and again during the three-month visit, "Who wanted to come to China?"

The money didn't last long. Income tax ate well over three-fourths of it. Although Hemingway also made a great deal in 1941, again income tax swallowed it.

With the United States' entry into World War II, Hemingway wanted to do his part in his own way. He set up a private intelligence network to ferret out spies in Cuba and report them to the American ambassador. His next scheme was to arm the *Pilar* as a Q-boat with bazookas, bombs, and machine guns. It would cruise the north coast pretending to carry scientists at work, but the crew would be on the lookout for German submarines.

Hemingway's sub-hunting voyages were actually well disguised fishing expeditions. Much drinking occurred on the *Pilar* and on shore after the hunts. Martha was getting disgusted with the drinking and with Hemingway's unkempt appearance. His customary garb included worn swimming trunks, a sweaty shirt, and no shoes. To get away, she accepted a *Collier's* assignment in the Caribbean, and Hemingway complained about her absence.

But when she was home, they argued—about his drinking, about his lack of bathing, about his exaggerating many of his experiences or straight lying about what he'd done. His bullying side took over more and more frequently. In one argument he yelled, "So you don't think I can write anymore. I'll show you, you conceited bitch. They'll be reading my stuff long after the worms have finished with you."

But when they were apart, she missed him. She worried about their marriage and wrote him,

> I wish we could stop it all now, the prestige, the possessions, the position, the knowledge, the victory. And by a miracle, return together under the arch at Milan, ... By God, how I wish it, ... the days hard, but with that shine on them from not being sure, but of hoping, of believing in fact in just the things we now so richly have.

Hemingway had been feeling much the same, but about a different time. He had been idealizing his life with Hadley and thinking of the Paris days when hope was a part of every day.

When *Collier's* assigned Martha to cover the war, she pleaded with Hemingway to go to Europe, too. They could be together as they'd been during the Spanish war. Hemingway was too caught up in his easy life and the admiration of the locals to forfeit it. He hadn't written anything noteworthy since *For Whom the Bell Tolls*, and that was eating at him, but he disguised it with false bravado. He planned a sub-hunting trip while Martha was on her European tour.

When Martha returned, she talked Hemingway into becoming a participant in the war. She had pulled strings with her Washington connections and told him if he would report on the Royal Air Force for an American magazine, the British would guarantee him a seat on a plane to London. His reputation would let him write for any magazine, but he chose *Collier's*, which was the one Martha had been writing for. With only one frontline correspondent allowed per magazine, he had put Martha out of a job. She was a second reporter for *Collier's* and not allowed on the plane. She crossed the Atlantic as the only passenger on a shipload of dynamite.

Hemingway flew to London. A few days later at lunch, he met *Time* reporter Mary Welsh and immediately asked her out. At their third meeting, he said "I don't know you, Mary, but I want to marry you."

She protested that they were both married, but he merely told her that the war might keep them apart, but to remember that he wanted to marry her.

Hemingway was famous in London, and everyone wanted to give him a party. After one party broke up around three in the morning, he hitched a ride to the hotel with another fellow who'd been drinking as much as he had. Their car ran head-on into a steel water tank. Hemingway's head smashed into the windshield, giving him a concussion and a deep cut in his scalp.

When Martha's ship arrived, reporters asked her about her husband's accident, but she knew nothing of it. She hurried to the hospital to find Hemingway holding court with friends, bottles of champagne and whiskey under the bed. He didn't look at all ill.

She'd had it with him and told him so. Her lonely trip on the dangerous boat had let her think of their differences, of his egotism, and of his bullying. From that point on she considered herself free of him, and he continued his courtship of Mary Welsh.

Hemingway's head injury delayed his firsthand observations of the Royal Air Force, but he was on a boat with other correspondents for the D-Day Invasion on June 6, 1944. Martha, without the proper frontline papers, stowed away onboard a hospital ship. She helped tend the wounded, and on the night of the seventh went ashore with stretcher bearers. Hemingway never forgave her for getting to France before him.

Although it was six weeks before Hemingway finally made it to France, he flew with the RAF on a bombing mission and loved the danger. In late July he hooked up with the Fourth Infantry Division and boasted to Mary in letters that he was serving on reconnaissance missions. Once he jumped from a motorcycle sidecar to avoid detection from Germans. He landed on boulders, injuring his head once again.

With the liberation of Paris next on the Allied agenda, Hemingway set himself up as an armed commander of a group of French partisans. His version of the triumphant entry into Paris was filled with adventure as he steered his group around enemy mines, tanks, and soldiers. Once inside the city he commandeered rooms at the Ritz, and the celebration began at the bar.

Soon Hemingway rejoined his earlier outfit, the Fourth Division, and watched them storm into Belgium. He was called back to headquarters to face an interrogation, since other journalists had turned him in for bearing arms and fighting in the war, a violation of the Geneva Convention. He gave reasonable explanations for taking off his press insignia and for helping with the partisans as a translator. Instead of owning weapons, he said he merely provided a storage place. He was cleared of all charges, but he felt horrible for committing perjury. Further bothering his mind were family matters. Martha wanted a divorce, and Bumby was missing-in-action.

He found a way to rejoin the Fourth Division and watched as they slogged their way toward Germany. It was a different set of circumstances than his hunts in Michigan, but the camaraderie among the men was the same. And when the officers and soldiers relaxed in the evening, Hemingway was the senior counselor. During offensives, Hemingway was cool under fire. When the regiment he was with suffered horrible casualties, Hemingway, sick with a severe cold, had seen enough of war and began negotiating a way back home.

He made one more trek to the front during the Battle of the Bulge. He settled the score with Martha, granting that he also wanted out of the marriage. He learned that Bumby was a prisoner of war, a step up from the missing-in-action report. And he convinced Mary to come to the Finca. Then he went home to Cuba.

WRITING IS A LONELY LIFE

During his absence, the Finca had not been maintained, so Hemingway set out to have it and himself restored before Mary arrived. He handed the house over to a large staff and talked to a doctor about the problems he'd had from the two concussions he'd suffered in Europe. The terrible headaches came and went, and his memory was impaired, resulting in a slowness of thought and speech. The doctor told him the bad gin he'd drunk in Europe was the worst thing for his head injuries.

Hemingway's new regimen was not to drink hard liquor until afternoon and only have a quarter bottle of wine with lunch. He swam, did lifting exercises, and played tennis to get in shape.

When Mary arrived in May, he seemed in much better health than when he'd left Europe. His spirits lifted with her presence and shot higher when Bumby was released from a German prisoner-of-war camp and came to the Finca to rest. Hemingway's other sons arrived for a vacation, and a holiday atmosphere prevailed.

Hemingway was driving Mary to the airport at the end of the month when the car skidded on a wet road. He hit his head on the rearview mirror, broke four ribs, and damaged a knee. Mary had facial cuts, and Hemingway carried her to the first aid station. Her trip to obtain a divorce from her husband was postponed while they both recovered. At the end of August, Mary flew to Chicago to get the divorce. Hemingway stayed in Cuba, since he needed six months of straight residence to apply for his own divorce from Martha, which was accomplished in December. He and Mary were married the following March.

Hemingway's writing had long been neglected. He had in mind a big book about the land, the sea, and the air, but it was in the thinking stage. He'd managed a few introductions to friends' books, but did not start on a new novel until the early months of 1946. By summer he'd written 1000 longhand pages of *The Garden of Eden*, an odd novel full of sexual overtones.

In August the Hemingways set off for a long car trip to Sun Valley. In a Wyoming motel room, Mary awoke with anguished pains. She had suffered an ectopic pregnancy and a Fallopian tube had ruptured. She hovered on the brink of death all day, and finally she had no pulse and her veins collapsed. A doctor told Hemingway to say goodbye to her.

Hemingway refused. He donned a gown and mask and convinced the doctor to cut an incision and locate a vein to administer mainline plasma. He administered the plasma himself until her pulse was restored. Her recovery took weeks, but by mid-September he moved her to Sun Valley, and after a couple weeks of rest, she joined his hunting expeditions for local game.

The hunting was good, but on the circuitous trip home through New York, Hemingway's dark side emerged. He despised negative criticism and, in public, verbally attacked a critic. He had called Hemingway one of the "hollow men" of literature. Hemingway's foul-mouthed retort did not endear him to those around him.

His mood brightened when he was awarded the Bronze Star for 'meritorious service' as a war correspondent in combat areas in World War II. Since grace under pressure was so important to him and courage signified manhood, he was thrilled with the award. He was also doing well financially as several of his short stories had received high-priced options for movies.

Physically, he was a wreck. His weight had topped out at 256 pounds, and his blood pressure was so high that he heard constant buzzing in his ears. He took an autumn trip to Windemere in Michigan to relive his youth, and then went on to Sun Valley. All along the way he watched his diet, and his weight and blood pressure came down.

Hemingway granted interviews to two reporters in 1948, one for *Life* and one for *The New Yorker*. He regaled them with his exploits in World War I, his skill in boxing and fishing, his dangerous submarine hunts in the *Pilar*, his strong sexual prowess, his hatred of his mother, and his belief that his father was a coward. He had built his reputation through his writing and he-man behavior. Now he had reporters willing to establish his legend in print.

His 49th birthday was celebrated onboard the *Pilar* with champagne from morning till night. It was the second long cruise of the summer, and he planned an even longer one for the fall—on a ship to Europe.

The Hemingways' boat docked in Italy, and they traveled to the places where he and Hadley had stayed long ago and where he had driven the ambulance in World War I. He visited the site of his wounding and buried a 1000-lire note in a hole in the ground, his own symbolism of giving both blood and money to Italy.

The couple stayed awhile north of Venice in a pleasant inn, where Hemingway worked on an article about the Gulf Stream in the morning, went duck shooting in the afternoon, and spent evenings relaxing in front of the open fireplace.

They decided to winter in Cortina. In December, Hemingway went partridge shooting with some new friends and met young Adriana Ivancich. Her noble upbringing, her gentle feminine manner, and her dark beauty attracted him immediately, even though she was one month shy of nineteen. Theirs was an innocent flirtation, but Hemingway once again had 'another woman' to love. Adriana was flattered by attention from the famous writer, and she showed him her schoolgirl drawings and confided that she wanted to be an artist.

She was the spark Hemingway needed to start another novel, this time a look back at World War II. He'd known the danger and exhilaration of war, he knew the terrain, and now he had the love interest to include.

His 50th birthday found him in Cuba and making headway on the book, *Across the River and Into the Woods*. He had hoped it would be finished before he returned to Europe six months later, but he carried it with him to Paris. There he was inspired to finish the book in a few days of writing nearly round the clock with only catnaps to rest his mind.

The Hemingways took their time seeing the countryside on the trip to Venice, relaxing here and there. Hemingway enjoyed sitting in front of a fire with friends, sipping gin and eating caviar. He wrote his publisher that "I corrupt easily, but in that sort of life I corrupt very fast."

In Venice he saw Adriana Ivancich once more, and the infatuation of the previous winter was still in his heart. He had even convinced Scribner's that she should illustrate the dust jacket of his new book. When the visit was over and he and Mary sailed for New York, he plunged into sadness.

Even at the Finca he could not shake his melancholy. Another accident aboard *Pilar* when he fell and hit his head, added to his dark mood. The headaches returned in full force.

With the visit of Adriana and her mother near the end of October 1950, Hemingway's mood once again swung high. He told her she inspired him to write, and he pounded out a book about the sea, one of three in a series that he envisioned with the same hero, Thomas Hudson. Then he began his now-famous novel *The Old Man and the Sea*, a story about an old man who hooks a giant marlin that pulls him out to sea. After his arduous battle with the marlin and the sea, he makes his way back to shore only to find that sharks had eaten most of his catch.

The words flowed despite Adriana's departure in early February 1951. Hemingway had heard the story from an old fisherman sixteen years earlier in Key West, but he'd never been able to write it until now.

Once it was finished, he started reshaping and cutting the sea book about an island in the stream. He told Scribner's that if something happened to him before he finished the big sea book with its several parts, they should publish the story about the old man and the sea as a stand-alone book, even though it would be a slender volume.

However, this premonition of death was not of his own. In 1951 Hemingway suffered tremendous losses with the deaths of his mother, his former wife Pauline, and his publisher Charles Scribner. Other friends around him were suffering ill health, but he was fine and fending off attempts of biographers, saying that he didn't want a biography written about him until he was dead.

Much of 1952 was taken up by cables and letters and contracts regarding *The Old Man and the Sea*. First it was published in its entirety in *Life*'s September 1 edition. Over five million copies of the magazine sold within 48 hours. Scribner's and the Book of the Month Club editions did very well. Critics raved about it. Readers sent letters; for three weeks after its release, Hemingway received 80 to 90 letters a day. Plans were underway for a movie. And the book won the Pulitzer Prize for fiction.

Hemingway wanted to celebrate. He'd dreamed of another trip to the Dark Continent, and now he set out on another African safari. Again, his first stop was Spain and the fiesta at Pamplona. From there the Hemingways traveled to Madrid, and Hemingway showed Mary exactly where the bridge was that he'd described in *For Whom the Bell Tolls*.

Hemingway had agreed to write a series of safari articles for *Look* magazine, and a photographer along with a friend from Cuba joined them in Africa. The safari troop, complete with guides, gun bearers, and other servants, set out the end of August 1953, and they were to be the sole game hunters in a reserve south of Nairobi, Kenya.

The four months of hunting were generally unsatisfactory. Hemingway did better shooting birds on the wing than he did the big game animals, although he did shoot a leopard, lion, zebra, and small game.

As a belated Christmas present for Mary, Hemingway had arranged a few days of flying over the African plains and the Nile River. Mary had snapped hundreds of pictures, but on the third day the pilot and plane dove to avoid a flock of birds and hit an abandoned telegraph wire.

The plane crashed on the rocky ground of Uganda. Hemingway suffered a sprained right shoulder, but otherwise the passengers were relatively unharmed. The radio was out, so they left the wreckage and spent a night huddled under the stars until the next day when they flagged down a boat on the river. By late afternoon they reached a small village.

Word had been received that the Hemingway plane had crashed. Another pilot flying over had seen the wreckage with no signs of survivors. Once found, a bush pilot had his 12-seater plane fueled at a primitive airport and was ready to take the Hemingways and their first pilot to Entebbe, Uganda.

The runway was an unpaved field. The plane bumped along, lifted, bumped down again, then stopped and burst into flames. Mary and the two pilots escaped through a window. Hemingway butted down a jammed door and jumped to safety. His scalp was bleeding and leaking clear fluid. Mary's knee was damaged.

They were taken by car to a hotel 50 miles away. The next morning a doctor appeared with bandages, and they were taken over 100 miles to

Entebbe. Hemingway talked to the press when they arrived, but was seeing double and his hearing came and went. When they were airlifted several days later to Nairobi, Kenya, he read his own obituaries from newspapers around the world that had been published when the press believed no one had survived the first crash.

His injuries were extensive. Besides a massive concussion, he suffered a ruptured liver, ruptured spleen, ruptured kidney, temporary loss of vision in his left eye and hearing in his left ear, a crushed vertebra, collapsed intestine, sprained right arm and shoulder and left leg, and first-degree burns on his head and arms. In Hemingway fashion, he told reporters he'd never felt better.

During his recovery, plans were made for a fishing trip off the coast of Kenya. Mary flew down to make arrangements while Hemingway stayed in Nairobi dictating a 15,000-word article for *Look*. When he felt a bit better, he went to the fishing camp, but rarely fished. A brushfire broke out, and he helped fight it, but was so physically weak that he fell into the flames and suffered second- and third-degree burns.

Hemingway, with renewed injuries, continued his recovery in Venice, where he stayed in bed in the hotel, received well-wishers, and gobbled pills. He was later driven to Spain and eventually returned to Cuba via ship. He and Mary had been gone nearly thirteen months.

Rumors had been circulating that he might win the Nobel Prize. But they were rumors that he had heard before, and therefore he didn't give them much credibility, going so far as to suggest that winning might be dangerous. His theory was that "no son of a bitch that ever won the Nobel Prize ever wrote anything worth reading afterwards." Despite his tough attitude, Hemingway was thrilled when he was awarded the Nobel Prize for his "powerful, style-making mastery of the art of modern narration." He told the Nobel committee that he was too ill to travel, but he wrote a speech for the award presentation that was read by the U.S. Ambassador to Sweden, John Cabot. In part, he wrote:

> Writing, at its best, is a lonely life. Organizations for writers palliate the writer's loneliness, but I doubt if they improve his writing. He grows in public stature as he sheds his loneliness and often his work deteriorates. For he does his work alone and if he is a good enough writer he must face eternity, or the lack of it, each day. For a true writer each book should be a new beginning where he tries again for something that is beyond attainment.

To escape all the publicity, he took trips on the Pilar, but he was in a great deal of pain. For the next two years, he recuperated. He and Mary visited Spain and then wintered in Paris in 1956, but he was under a doctor's care much of that time. When it came time to leave the Ritz hotel, porters told him there were two more of his trunks in the basement that had been stored there since 1928. They held some old clothes and some of Hemingway's writing from the early years in Paris.

Back in Cuba, Hemingway set to work on his memoirs of those Paris years. From the fall of 1957 to the spring of 1958, he wrote sketches of the people he'd known in France. Then he pulled out *The Garden of Eden*, the book he'd started years earlier, and worked on it.

Living in Cuba was becoming hard; an underground rebel group tried to overthrow the dictator Fulgencio Batista. At four o'clock one morning, soldiers searched the Finca for a rebel fugitive. They didn't bother Hemingway's multitude of pet cats, but they shot his dog. He kept silent, but only because he would be in peril if he spoke up.

He vowed not to spend the summer in the turbulent place, and he and Mary drove to Ketchum, Idaho, near the Sun Valley resort. They stayed through mid-March, missing the Cuban revolution led by Fidel Castro.

The Hemingways were briefly in Cuba before leaving for Spain in 1959. Hemingway celebrated his 60th birthday at a big party in that country, but some of the guests thought he was verbally cruel to Mary. During that dangerous summer, he spent time following the bullfighting contests between two leading matadors. He was writing an article on the competition for *Life*, so stayed in the country until mid-October. He returned briefly to Cuba, then set out for Idaho in November.

His behavior was getting more and more belligerent toward his friends and toward Mary. But he began working again as soon as he returned to Cuba in January. His 10,000-word article for *Life* expanded to 120,000 words, and he needed help to cut it to a reasonable amount for magazine publication. He felt he must return to Spain again to gather up loose ends, but the trip by plane in August was an endurance flight for him.

He arrived with the air of a depressed man. Fear, loneliness, insomnia, and a failed memory plagued him. Nightmares haunted his dreams when he could sleep. He feared a nervous breakdown.

By October 1960, Hemingway was back in Idaho, a shadow of his former self. He seemed fragile, quiet, and spoke in spurts, not in full sentences. Something had to be done. Mary convinced him to see doctors at the Mayo Clinic. He was no longer in control of his life or his mind.

Initial physical tests revealed mild diabetes and an enlarged liver from years of alcoholic consumption. Worse was his mental state. Doctors believed shock treatments would help his severe depression and paranoia, although the treatments temporarily took his memory. He was released from the hospital after 53 days and returned to Idaho. Here he worked at arranging the sketches in his Paris memoir, but seemed to accomplish little. He stared out the window and seemed to see nothing.

He wrote nothing and cried because words wouldn't come. His despair led him to hold a loaded gun to his head. If he couldn't write, he didn't want to live. Mary quickly had him whisked back to the Mayo clinic. There he endured more shock treatments and was dismissed in June. Mary thought it was a mistake. He was delusional, but he was sly and cunning and presented one side of his personality to the doctors and quite another to her.

The road trip home to Idaho took five long days. On his second morning in his Idaho retreat, he took the key to the basement storage room where the guns were locked. He selected a familiar double-barreled shotgun and climbed the stairs. In the entryway he loaded it and placed the butt of the gun on the floor, leaned forward until the barrels touched his head, and pulled the triggers.

Ernest Hemingway was dead by his own hand at the age of 61.

ISOBEL O'DONNELL

Hemingway's Secret Codes: Revealing a Passion for Culture and Language

Hemingway was a journalist, a writer, and a sportsman. The author used his experiences with hunting, fishing, bullfighting, and soldiering as back-grounds and for cultural depth in many of his stories. He writes about the human struggle with love, loss, separation, isolation, and politics. In some of his best works, like *The Sun Also Rises* and "Hills Like White Elephants," many of his characters are imbued with subtle characteristics that show their complex relationship to the world around them, exhibiting a cultural sensitivity that became his trademark. Critical consideration of his work reveals that Hemingway was a complex subject engendering much positive criticism as well as detailed analyses of his weaknesses. Hemingway, however, proves to be as enduring a force in literature as he was a complex individual in his life and his art. His best writing is powerful; he has an uncanny ability to reveal things by implication. This ability to maintain the reader's interest by not telling every detail appeals to and enhances the reader's imaginative powers.

Santiago, the fisherman hero of *The Old Man and the Sea* has a fishing style that parallels Hemingway's writing style. The author reels us in with his verbal acuity that reflects linguistic and cultural intonation. Envision the old fisherman in a small boat; he has hooked a fish so large that it is pulling the boat and the old man out to sea. The old man must give out fishing line when the line is so taut that it reaches its breaking point. And then when the fish tires and the tension falters, the man must take up the slack. Hemingway's method of writing is like an old man carefully letting the line out on a big fish; consequently, we are slowly let in on the events that drive and reveal the characters, the story, and the situation.

advice to maestro.

53

Santiago feels bad about killing his brother ↑

The *Old Man and the Sea* is reminiscent of Coleridge's *The Rime of the Ancient Mariner*; both are poetic stories of men at sea. The ancient mariner, unlike Santiago, commits an act "in contempt of the laws of hospitality"[1] by killing an albatross, a bird that has visited his ship and come at the mariner's calls for nine days. The ancient mariner tells his story with much regret. Realizing his error, he repents, but is haunted by his crime against nature. The Mariner experiences a deeply spiritual change and comes to love "all things both great and small."[2] Santiago's worst crime is that he is unlucky, *salao*, "the worst kind of unlucky." The sail he flies is tattered and "patched with flour sacks." On the first page, Hemingway tells us that it looks like the flag of "permanent defeat." But Santiago never shows deep moral affliction, as does the ancient mariner. Of course Santiago regrets having killed the marlin because the sharks destroyed it and it was, therefore, a waste of life. But Hemingway's old man had no cause for a deeper sense of penitence; his original intention was to catch fish to support himself, after all, he was a fisherman. But the ancient mariner's killing of the albatross was uncalled for and brought misery and regret that resulted in a religious vision. The motivation for Santiago's misery is not as deep; he is poor, old, and unlucky at the start and at the end of the story. Santiago's character does not contain the sharp characterization and complex relation to the world that we see in earlier novels and short stories.

The epigraph to Coleridge's work could almost be Hemingway's literary credo as well as a description of his style: "I readily believe that there are more invisible than visible Natures in the universe....The human mind has always sought the knowledge of these things, but never attained it … at the same time we must be watchful for the truth and keep a sense of proportion, so that we may distinguish the certain from the uncertain, day from night."[3] Hemingway strove to write "one true sentence" and he believed that the writing was like an iceberg—only a fraction of it was visible, the rest implied. In works like "A Clean Well-Lighted Place," "The Killers," and "The Undefeated," despite the thorough description of the action, the reader is left to grapple with the complex issues of suicide, contract murder, and desperation, because the emotive details are not explained in any way.

Hemingway crystallizes events and characters through dialogue. His dialogue is effective in slowly revealing situations and characters while at the same time concealing much about the characters so that curiosity is piqued, making the reader study passages for clarification. With Hemingway's most intriguing work, the reader wants to catch all the clues and subtleties. Our interest in the story is enhanced as the sparse dialogue and prose build tension and interest in the story. The difficulty with Hemingway's carefully allotted, often monosyllabic dialogue is the possibility that the repetition can become monotonous. There are times in *The Old Man and the Sea* that the old man repeats phrases and thoughts to a point of tedium for the reader. Santiago is the only character for much of the book, and it is problematic for a writer to sustain interest in a solo situation.

Hemingway uses dialogue and narration to reveal the subtleties of character. He uses simple language and, through it, he often reveals complex psychological situations. Santiago's monologue (*The Old Man and the Sea*) leaves us looking for more about Santiago, why he is compelled to go after the big fish, to risk his life. Is he just in the moment battling with his "brother," the fish, whom he must kill? He talks to himself both out loud and through internal monologue. He talks to his brother, the big fish, and to the birds. Hemingway reveals characters and situations through insight gained from this dialogue. He snares us with his piercing prose that revolves around descriptions of immediate sensations: the old man faint with hunger and thirst, the pain in his rope burned hands and back, the satisfaction of eating the raw tuna.

Hemingway's simple language is perfect for describing immediate sensation. French critics praise him for his down-to-earth, American simplicity. His direct style belied a complexity that gave the colloquial American, monosyllabic dialogue and prose new dignity. In his essay on Malraux and Hemingway, Ben Stoltzfus describes similarities and differences between Andre Malraux, French Statesman and writer, and Hemingway. Malraux comments on the phenomenon of the American writer who writes simply, saying, "To my mind, the essential characteristic of contemporary American writing is that it is the only literature whose creators are not intellectuals."[4] Ben Stoltzfus points out that Malraux:

> … wondered how American literature could intellectualize itself without losing its direct approach. It was precisely this direct approach that French writers and critics such as Jean-Paul Sartre, Albert Camus, and Claude-Edmonde Magny had admired.

Even though admired by French critics, Hemingway's "direct" style was not always appreciated by English and American critics. Not only was Hemingway's language simple but he was censured for his use of four letter words, a prominent feature in several of his writings.

Hemingway was very sure of himself when it came to profanity. He felt that certain words were necessary to create the atmosphere of the book. Hemingway's publisher had difficulty with the obscenity he peppered throughout his work. His editor, Maxwell Perkins at Scribner's, had to fight for the books in question to be approved.[5] Perkins managed to convince

Scribner's that *The Sun Also Rises* was of such consequence that it had to be published. The author cut all he could but refused to remove the word "bitch" from the book. Hemingway writes to Perkins regarding final revisions:

> 96 Rue Froidevaux,
> Paris, France.
> August 21, 1926
>
> Dear Mr. Perkins,
> I imagine we are in accord about the use of certain <u>words</u> and I never use a word without first considering if it is replaceable. But in the proof I will go over it all very carefully. I have thought of one place where Mike when drunk and wanting to insult the bull-fighter keeps saying—tell him bulls have no balls. That can be changed—and I believe with no appreciable loss to—bulls have no horns. But in the matter of the use of the Bitch by Brett—I have never once used this word ornamentally nor except when it was absolutely necessary and I believe the few places where it is used must stand...[6]
>
> Yours Always,
> Ernest Hemingway

Despite all these precautions, *The Sun Also Rises* was banned in Boston. But Perkins and Hemingway had labored over the words so carefully that they knew outrage was probable if not unavoidable. In fact Perkins was inundated with letters from people who were shocked that Scribner's would publish works that "[pandered] to the public's basest tastes."[7] The author felt justified in his reasons for using the offending words. Hemingway wrote Perkins later in the same letter, "I think that words—and I will cut anything I can—that are used in conversation in *The Sun* etc. are justified by the tragedy of the story. But of course I haven't seen it for some time and not at all in type." So Hemingway was aware of the problems caused by profanity but exercised his artistic judgment and determined when they were called for and when not. Since the author indicates that such language is representative of the tragedy in the story then the language does not bring to the characters a greatness or a toughness, but rather a diminishment, which is what *The Sun Also Rises* is really about, a diminishment that has implications for the entire human race in the aftermath of the devastation of WWI.

But after Perkins had passed his concerns about obscenity and libel onto Hemingway, the author decided to continue cutting the manuscript. So it was that Hemingway decided to cut the first 15 pages of *The Sun Also Rises*. He tells Perkins in a letter:

> I believe that, in the proofs, I will start the book at what is now page 16 I the Mss. There is nothing in those first sixteen pages that does not come out, or is explained, or restated in the rest of the book—or is unnecessary to state. I think it will move much faster from the start that way.[8]

Perkins managed to convince him not to do this since this opening section served as an introduction to Robert Cohn and set the scene for the expatriots. Cutting it would have plunged the reader, at the outset, into the scene of Jake's dinner with the French whore, Georgette. The scene is not without rewards. It introduces us to a minor Hemingway woman who is not idealized and is definitely interesting, albeit a somewhat grotesque figure with "bad teeth." Generally his heroines range from fairly well drawn to insufficiently developed. When Hemingway's heroines are created as the love interest, they become idealized and appear without the personal traits that might have made them interesting.

Hemingway's male characters are often convincing and full of life. *The Nick Adams Stories* offer an intriguing protagonist who attempts to respond to the paradoxes of life. In "The Killers" Nick seems lightly sketched at first, then moves into responding to the threat against Ole Andreson, boxer. Nick's reaction is to try alerting Andreson, believing that there must be something the retired boxer can do to avoid being killed. But Andreson's attitude is that there is no way out. He is resigned to waiting for the killers, and can't see any purpose in trying to get away. Nick is hemmed in by his awareness of the impending murder, he "can't stand to think about [Ole Andreson] waiting in the room and knowing he's going to get it." Nick finds it "too damned awful." He has an overwhelming awareness of the events and has participated in them to some extent. He is uneasy with his connection to this "awful" event. Unlike Ole, Nick wants to get away from the horror of the murder and his response to the situation is very different than George's. George wants to pretend it didn't happen and says, "you better not think about it." The brilliant juxtaposition of Andreson's resignation, Nick's horror and George's denial helps create complex and subtly interwoven characters in a few pages.

Contrary to this, in *A Farewell to Arms*, Hemingway's characterization of women, and the English nurse Catherine Barkley in particular, is not as effective. She is a Hemingway accessory, not fully fleshed out. She is not adequately revealed through dialogue and there is a great lack of background information. A brief conversation introduces her father simply as a man with gout who will die before Frederic Henry will ever meet him. Henry's own family background is scant but his character comes alive through dialogue and action. Once Catherine becomes a love object her individuality evaporates with her credibility. Barkley is not a convincing character when compared to D. H. Lawrence's Lady Chatterly or Gustave Flaubert's Emma Bovary. Both Flaubert and Lawrence put their heroines in difficult situations, but one has the feeling that despite fate and passion, these women ultimately make choices for their own reasons. Constance Chatterly and Emma have a morally questionable choice to make, which is what makes them interesting. Hemingway has not created dilemmas, moral problems, or choices for Catherine, as he did for the hero, Frederic Henry. Philip Young says this about Barkley:

> Memorable too, in her devotion and her ordeal—though much less memorable, and much less real—is Henry's English mistress. Idealized past the fondest belief of most people, and even the more realistic wishes of some, compliant, and bearing unmistakable indications of the troubles to come when she will appear as mistress of heroes to come, Catherine Barkley has at least some character in her own right, and is both the first true "Hemingway heroine," and the most convincing one.[9]

Other female characters like Pilar and the antiheroine Brett Ashley in *The Sun Also Rises* are solid, self-directed women. Pilar, a fascinating Hemingway character, the "ugly" woman, lives, loves and fights for her ideals. Pilar is part gypsy and reads Jordan's palm; she is deemed "a witch" and her band of guerillas respect and reinforce her magical craft. Brett is referred to as Circe, the goddess who turned Odysseus' men into swine. Brett's sexual magic turns Mike and Robert Cohn into lost, lonely animals: Jake of course is immune to her, as Odysseus was to Circe. Brett represents an archetypal force like the Temple prostitute, or Salmacis, the nymph whose fountain waters emasculated men who swam there. Brett is powerful and had she ever gotten sober she would have taken over the novel. In *The Sun Also Rises*, Hemingway is careful to keep each character locked into the hierarchy of the novel so that the plot can function effectively, leading to an utter lack of change and the hopelessness exhibited by these characters who are casualties of war. Pilar is allowed more room and expression, probably because she is not Jordan's love interest.

In *Farewell to Arms* the narrow scope of dialogue allotted to Catherine Barkley is insufficient to evoke real character. Perhaps her repetitive remarks such as, "You see, I do anything you want," and "There isn't any me anymore. Just what you want..." represent her great love for Henry and her relief from the heartbreak and craziness at the loss of her fiancée in the battle of the Somme. Yet her words inadequately convey this. When reaching for a deeper sense of her complexity the reader is thwarted. She becomes more and more of a repetitious, leech-like appendage to Frederic Henry. This shallow characterization indicates that Barkley has annihilated her individuality and become part of Henry. This character weakness does work favorably to enhance the depth of Henry's tragedy at the end. When Catherine dies, we are not terribly moved, but what is moving is that we feel a large part of Henry dies at the end with her. Had she been fully fleshed out and real to us, she might have upstaged Henry's desperation. Had we known her better, her death might have become the melodramatic focus and the story would have become her story. But the story Hemingway wrote was about Henry, from beginning to end. Hemingway's heroes never learned to share the stage with women, if they had, his novels would have been completely different, perhaps better.

Hemingway is masterful with his staccato dialogue in the short story, "Hills Like White Elephants" creating a female character who is interesting and has opinions, although she may not have the final say in her destiny and her impending abortion. The girl, Jig, makes a comment to the man about the hills in the distance. She says, "They look like white elephants." The man is uncomfortable with the implication of the statement. The white hills look like fertility symbols. The couple begins drinking and the girl says, "... I said the mountains looked like white elephants. Wasn't that bright?" The man replies with the same sarcasm, "That was bright." And then the man describes the procedure she will undergo, "It's really an awfully simple operation, Jig… It's not really an operation at all… It's just to let the air in." The girl asks him what will happen afterwards, whether they'll be happy. He replies in the affirmative and states that he's known lots of people who have done it. Jig then say, "So have I … and afterward they were all so happy." The girl holds up her end of this awful discussion, yet she seems resigned to what the man insists is right, the abortion. She says, "But if I do it, then it will be nice again if I say things are like white elephants, and you'll like it?" The story is masterful and is always fresh with each rereading. We know no background information on the girl and yet her attitude, observations, and sarcasm create an entire human being who is angry, fearful, and trapped by her desire for "things to be like they were." Hemingway paints a bleak, amoral world where people are trapped by "the good times." The story is effective because there is not only a hero, but a credible woman struggling against him, defining his shallow and selfish desire to have only Jig (but not a child), thereby authorizing the abortion as the only plausible solution.

In *For Whom the Bell Tolls*, *A Farewell to Arms*, *The Sun Also Rises*, and *The Old Man and the Sea*, Hemingway creates a peculiar brand of prose and dialogue. Since these stories take place in non-English speaking countries, he uses a smattering of foreign words as well as using verbatim translations of them to effect a change in thinking in the reader, an initiation into a new world. Any one who speaks another language knows the traps of using "translated" phrases that keep the original sense of the foreign word. Such verbatim translations produce an awkward kind of English that tells a lot about the speaker's origins, culture and way of thinking. Take for example the very comical scene in *The Sun Also Rises* where Jake and Bill have gone fishing. They discuss the wine they are drinking. Bill says, "Let us utilize the fowls of the air. Let us utilize the product of the vine." A little later Jake hands him another bottle and says, "Here, utilize a little of this." Later they initiate the Englishman Harris, who is staying at their hotel, and Jake narrates that "He had taken up utilizing from Bill." The French verb *utiliser* means to use or to make use of and Hemingway writes stilted conversation that creates a special joke shared by Jake, Bill, and Harris. Another instance in the same novel is the scene where Georgette the prostitute dances on the crowded dance floor. She says, "My God, what a box to sweat in!" *Boîte* in English means box, but in French it is the idiomatic term for nightclub. Hemingway chooses the verbatim translation, in my mind, because it indicates that they are speaking French, since it is unlikely that the prostitute speaks English. It also adds an exotic flavor to the novel that is very effective.

In *For Whom the Bell Tolls*, the conversation is mostly in Spanish and Hemingway does a fine job of "translating" and keeping the feel of Spanish as well as sprinkling Spanish words throughout, letting the reader feel a part of the scene. He uses his words wisely, Pablo says, "Vaya, a day commences," and the response by Pilar, "Now let us go and get coffee." This was spoken in Spanish and the translation has the effect of foreign language replete with idiom and accent, yet Hemingway used only a few words and slight syntactical/grammatical emphasis to make it understood. He deals effectively with the problems that dialogue presents and he uses English and foreign languages like a secret code that provides an entrée into the heart of a culture offering us access to new experiences.

In *The Sun Also Rises*, when Jake meets Montoya in Pamplona, he shares a special interest with him. Montoya acknowledges that Jake shares his *aficion* for bullfighting. Jake tells us, "Aficion means passion. An aficionado is one who is passionate about the bullfights. All the good bullfighters stayed at Montoya's hotel; that is, those with aficion stayed there." There are often coteries in Hemingway's work, and it is usually desirable to understand them enough to gain a level of superiority that comes from feeling apart from or better than the rest of the crowd. Montoya represents the best of the bullfighting coterie. Jake describes him this way:

> He smiled again. He always smiled as though bullfighting were a very special secret between the two of us; a rather shocking but really very deep secret that we knew about. He always smiled as though there were something lewd about the secret to outsiders, but that it was something that we understood. It would not do to expose it to people who would not understand.

Hemingway, Jake, and the reader, always want to be with the people in the know—to be part of the clique. Only special people can understand aficion. Foreigners in general and English-speaking people in particular are not able to pass the aficion test. But Jake does, and the reader can, vicariously. In this way we rise to a level above the rest, for Jake it makes him a little better than his traveling companions. For the reader there is the excitement from having access to new cultural codes, and being given the clues to crack them. Later in the book, it is the American, Jake, who sits down to talk aficion shop with the bullfighter Romero. Through this exchange and others like it, Hemingway initiates the reader even further. He compliments us by letting us be in this special club. While Jake and Romero have drinks with a bullfight critic we get our next lesson in aficion:

> [Romero] was anxious to know the word for *Corrida de toros*, the exact translation. Bullfight he was suspicious of. I explained that bullfight in Spanish was the *lidia* of a *toro*. The Spanish word corrida means in English the running of bulls—the French translation is *Course de taureaux*. The critic put that in. There is no Spanish word for bullfight.

The aficion here, is Hemingway's, and it's all about language that represents the moral codes involved in the bullfighting coterie and the Anglo expatriate coterie. It is of great importance that the word bullfight does not exist in Spanish, and especially that Romero, a *lidiador*, who knows several phrases of English is "suspicious" of it. The implication is that the word "bullfight" degrades, or perhaps subverts the true passion of the activity. *Lidia* means fight, contest, or battle, so the meaning of the word in Spanish (according to Romero's reaction) must be more like contest or battle, implying a certain expertise or sportsmanship. Hemingway offered the world this kind of culture through his intense study of words and their cultural associations. One could call this type of literary expression "cultural etymology." Whether telling a story about an abortion ("Hills Like White Elephants") or a bunch of drunken, ruined expatriates (*The Sun Also Rises*), or the Spanish *afición* for the *lidia* of a *toro*, Hemingway gives us words that have the descriptive digging power to activate the past, present, and future of the character, infusing him with cultural and personal qualities we know to be real, because they are explained with keywords in Spanish, French, Italian, and English. In the 21st century the personal has become political, what we wear, eat, buy, etc. makes a political statement because our role as consumer supports the larger structures that control us. With Hemingway, the cultural is personal, and this is one of the reasons he has endured. He was able to convey cultural subtleties through his writing, filling his books with many vivid characters and sentiments. He strove to write "one true sentence." Superficially, many of those sentences were very simple, monosyllabic even. What Hemingway meant by "one true sentence" may have been a construction that reflected cultural etymology rolling forward in time to create a complex personal experience, one where the reader experiences the fictional character and has a personal reaction or connection established to the character. Trilling speaks of Hemingway's style in his essay on *For Whom the Bell Tolls*:

> With the themes that bring out his craft most happily, Hemingway has never been so good—no one else can make so memorable the events of physical experience; how things look, and move, and are related to each other. From the beginning of the novel to the end, one has the happy sense of the author's unremitting and successful poetic effort. So great is this effort, indeed, that one is inclined to feel that it is at times even too great, that it becomes conscious of itself....

Yet even in a self-conscious work one must consider the powerful event that occurs when he is able to evoke the worlds of the expatriate, the French prostitute and Spanish guerillas. *For Whom the Bell Tolls* may have failed on several levels, as Trilling astutely points out, but what Hemingway does with his cultural etymology is something more than a "poetic effort." There is in Hemingway a sense of pasts and futures rolling in and pulling back like waves on a shore. And in this tidal *mêlée* Hemingway gives us the keys to structure, plot, and cultural meeting points that evoke humans dealing with external forces, like war, as well as internal emotions and dilemmas. *For Whom the Bell Tolls* is not as unified as *The Sun Also Rises*, but it does exhibit Hemingway's power revealing life, culture, and the emotive elements through his 'translated' Spanish dialogue with Pablo's band of guerillas. In this book, Hemingway brings to life a vast array of characters, many of whom exhibit inner life. The idealizing of the romance between Jordan and Maria is problematic; the heroic one-man standoff at the end is unappealing in its lack of subtlety. However, the many minor characters, like Pilar, Pablo, El Sordo, and even the impulsive gypsy Rafael fill the book with memorable events, reactions, and methods of Spanish cursing.

In his works, Hemingway offers us this linguistic lineage, and in so doing he creates a sense of time rolling in and pulling back like waves on a shore, sometimes hiding the shoreline, sometimes revealing it. He uses this same technique repeatedly in his writing, barely communicating the meaning of a scene except by inference. Then he exposes a detail that has a revelatory impact and offers an intuitive moment for the reader, mildly reminiscent of the epiphanies of James Joyce in works like "The Dead" and "Araby." Hemingway echoes this by initiating the reader into the world of drunken war casualties and bullfighting in *The Sun Also Rises*; although it is something quite different than the calculated building-up of characters through environment that Joyce uses in his short stories. Joyce describes the Irish-Catholic towns, the priests, the schools, but we do not have a sense that we are a part of it. Joyce keeps the reader at a distance and builds his story in a biting way. Hemingway's narrators are personable and they offer us clues to the culture; we can become insiders. Hemingway gives out what he considers to be the *truth* of the situation; he invites the reader to be part of that world. His narrators are often first person and cannot know everything; therefore much is revealed through dialogue and action. In his third-person works like "The Killers" and "A Clean Well-Lighted Place" to name a few, the case is often the similar, much is revealed through action, dialogue, and the impact of Hemingway's sensitivity to the language. His power lies in smallness; his power is a kind of truth that shines a light for a second so we get a glimpse and then are left in the darkness with the image echoing in our minds, hungering for more information.

Hemingway creates palpable moods with his descriptive prose. Many of his most memorable scenes are descriptions of nature, passion, cafés, eating, drinking, fishing, and bullfighting. He impresses us with vivid scenes whether in a hospital bed, a sleeping bag, under the spell of a woman or under fire. *The Sun Also Rises* describes the mood of post-WWI on many levels. The loss of human life was inconceivable at the time. The new killing technology made possible larger numbers of casualties than ever before. The machine gun, a new implement of destruction, made its war-debut in WWI. The concept that war was won by strategy or generals or moral superiority, died a fast death. It appeared that good could not prevail anymore. The moral approach to war is that one's will, spirit, and cause will create a positive outcome. But the devastation of this war effectively terminated the days "when people believed in something," and the spirit of this human and moral blackout is brought to light in *The Sun Also Rises.*

In *A Farewell to Arms*, we are told that Catherine Barkley's fiancé was killed in the Battle of the Somme that occurred on July 1, 1916. This early battle brought the largest one-day loss, to date, in the history of the British and Empire Armies. Armed with machine guns, enemies were able to mow down opponents as they charged. Several well-manned machine guns with many rounds of ammunition could mutilate and kill hundreds and hundreds of men. As a result, a common sight in Britain after the war was the amputee veteran on the street corner. Within the first few hours of fighting, the British and Empire armies suffered over 60,000 casualties of which included 20,000 dead. This was the war where morality and God evaporated under the siege of advanced weapons technology.

Hemingway seizes upon these feelings of loss, desperation, and hopelessness in *The Sun Also Rises.* The reader is informed of the depth and horror of the war events through the description and dialogue of this *"génération perdue."* In *A Moveable Feast*, Hemingway's posthumous memoir, Gertrude Stein elaborates on this phrase used by the boss at the gas station,

> [Miss Stein] had some ignition trouble with the old Model T Ford she then drove and the young man who worked in the garage and had served in the last year of the war had not been adept, or perhaps had not broken the priority of other vehicles, in repairing Ms. Stein's Ford. Anyway he had not been *sérieux* and had been corrected severely by the patron of the garage after Miss Stein's protest. The patron had said to him, "You are all a *génération perdue.*"
>
> "That's what you are. That's what you all are," Miss Stein said. "All of you young people who served in the war. You are a lost generation…. You have no respect for anything. You drink yourselves to death…."

Hemingway later says, in a gruffly tolerant way, "…the hell with her lost-generation talk and all the dirty, easy labels." He has a point, there is something reductive in the label; it doesn't say enough. The appalling repercussions of WWI need a larger form of expression, such as the novel Hemingway wrote. *The Sun Also Rises* is an excellent example of his ability to reveal by concealing. He never says much about the war; he shows its effect on the bodies, minds, and souls of his characters. Jake is impotent from a war wound, and because of this Jake and Brett's mutual love is never consummated. These characters are plagued with problems and Hemingway shows this through a party atmosphere where the standard line is "have another drink." But none of this is social drinking—these characters drink to survive their awful days and lonely nights; to forget their problems that Hemingway ironically reveals through abundant drinks, drunkenness, sexual promiscuity, and parties.

Hemingway also uses his descriptive dialogue to echo these larger themes: the isolation and loneliness of existence, the meaninglessness of life and the daily struggle. *The Sun Also Rises* gives us a look into the desperation, alcoholism, and loss of faith in these casualties of WWI. Jake and Brett are in love with each other but Brett sleeps with Robert Cohn, who ends up in love with her. The unenviable Mike is Brett's fiancé; he hightails it out of Spain when Brett indulges herself with the young bullfighter Romero. Bill Gorton, Jake's friend, provides much drunken humor and is a foil for Jake. Brett's active sex life underscores Jake's impotence. Hemingway has neatly and subtly plotted a work where fishing scenes, Brett's sex thrills, Robert Cohn's and Romero's virility, all lead us back to Jake's desperate scenario. He is unable to satisfy the woman he loves and he acts as procurer for her, going along with her "engagement" to Mike and enabling her affair with Romero.

Brett is drunk, unsatisfied, and in love with Jake. Hemingway fills in her character with appealing qualities (other than her much-remarked upon beauty). The author shows Brett's excitement and morbid curiosity at the bullfights; she seems to have courage when she's vaguely sober. Brett typifies the wartime cliché of sexual immediacy when death is all around. But the war is over and Brett is another of the wounded like all those of this "lost generation." She is impulsive. She decides to marry Mike, then to leave him for the bullfighter, Romero, and then runs back to Jake for help when it all falls apart. Brett Ashley is like a rat running in a wheel till she's exhausted, pauses to get her strength up, and then keeps going. Hemingway portrays this meaningless existence without discernible format, plan, or symbol. He just lets the novel happen in dialogue. The story could have been the story of any group of friends out having a good time. It is masterful in its simplicity. The philosophizing found in *For Whom the Bell Tolls* and the overemphasis on symbol in *A Farewell to Arms* are absent in *The Sun Also Rises*. In *For Whom the Bell Tolls*, Hemingway relies on interior monologues to reveal Jordan's feelings and it is not as effective as the showing of character through action. In *A Farewell to Arms* the rain emerges as a glaring symbol of death early on and is often repeated, even told to us by Catherine Barkley who said to Frederic Henry that she saw them together "dead in the rain." In *The Sun Also Rises* you never have the sense that Hemingway has planted directions or indicators to enforce plot, mood, or meaning; the lack of commentary lets the action and dialogue reveal the characters and events. Even when the narrator, Jake, intrudes with his emotions, he does not overwhelm the story. He stays in the background, enhancing the overall effect of desperation and loss.

For Whom the Bell Tolls is the story of Robert Jordan, an American dynamiter in the midst of the Spanish Civil War. He fights for the Republican Cause and he is in Spain for three days. His purpose is to blow up a bridge in order to foil supply lines for the Fascists during a surprise attack by the Republicans. His life among the band of guerillas in the mountains is interesting, romantic, and dangerous. Robert Jordan is a *partizan*, the narrator defines this term:

> Because of our mobility and because we did not have to stay afterwards to take the punishment we never knew how anything really ended, he thought. You stayed with a peasant and his family. You came at night and ate with them. In the day you were hidden and the next night you were gone. You did your job and cleared out. The next time you came that way you heard that they had been shot. It was as simple as that.
>
> But you were always gone when it happened. The *partizans* did their damage and pulled out.

Jordan, of course, will be the American *partizan* that doesn't get out. Hemingway ensures his hero status by reversing the rule. In the end the Spanish guerillas and his love, Maria, get out on horseback and he stays behind, mortally wounded, machine gun poised, ready to take on the fascists. Hemingway creates a hero who did more than finish "the job and clear out."

Carlos Baker in his article, "The Spanish Tragedy" argues for the tragic epic nature of *For Whom the Bell Tolls*:

> If *For Whom the Bell Tolls* is a kind of epic, it is above all a tragic epic. Like the *Iliad*, it may be seen as a study in doom, Madrid, like Troy, was fated to fall. Seventeen months of hind-[250/251] sight on the Spanish war helped to mature in Hemingway a feeling that the Republican defeat had been virtually inevitable....
>
> ...The struggle could not seem to be hopeless. Yet, as a study in doom, the novel must early isolate and dramatize those adverse powers and power-failures which would ultimately combine to defeat the Spanish republic.[10]

Baker goes on to point out the internal dangers such as Pablo, leader of the guerilla band, who exhibits cowardice and defeatism. Pablo is always drunk, has nightmares, and wishes he could bring back the many people he has killed. He doesn't care about politics anymore: he just wants to retire on the wealth of his stolen horses. Pilar, his woman, accuses him of becoming a capitalist, another betrayal of her communist ideals. Baker considers the elements of doom: the dangerously inefficient bureaucracy, the "Spanish temperament," Commander Golz's lack of power to fight the war properly, and Rafael, the gypsy, who leaves his guard post to shoot rabbits.[11] Baker considers these and other elements and themes as contributing to the nature of tragic epic in *For Whom the Bell Tolls.*

Lionel Trilling, however, sees this book on the Spanish Civil War as missing the tragic mark, he argues:

> …Hemingway, we may be sure, intended that the star-crossed love and heroic death of Robert Jordan should be a real tragedy, a moral and political tragedy which would suggest and embody the tragedy of the Spanish war. In this intention he quite fails. The clue to the failure is the essential inner dullness of his hero. Robert Jordan does not have within himself what alone could have made tragedy out of this remarkable melodrama—he does not in himself embody the tensions which were in the historical events he lived through. His fate is determined by the moral and political contradictions of the historical situation, but he himself explicitly refuses to recognize these contradictions, he stands apart from them. And since it is Jordan's fate that must provide whatever intellectual architectonic the novel is to have, the novel itself [640/641] fails, not absolutely but relatively to its possibility and to its implied intention.[12]

The Aristotelian tragic hero's misfortune is brought about by an error in his judgment and the result of this is a downward spiral from happiness to misery. When Trilling speaks of Jordan's inner dullness, I think more of his uprightness. He never seems to make the actual mistake in judgment that causes his downfall. But Jordan neglected to send word to Goltz as soon as he saw the problem with Pablo's drunkenness and despair and Jordan was too captivated with Maria to think straight. But none of these errors constitute the actual cause for his death, as Trilling indicates. And he never really sinks into a downward spiral because he is still gungho at the thought of staving off the fascists to protect his escaping guerillas, and Maria. Those responsible for the death of Jordan are the bureaucrats running the war. Trilling blames André Marty, the deluded and paranoid officer who delays delivery of the dispatch from Jordan to Goltz informing him that the attack is no longer a surprise, that it should be called off. This delay not only causes the needless death of Jordan and most of the guerillas, but also makes a tragic sacrifice of the Republican troops who will walk into a deathtrap, erroneously thinking they have the element of surprise. At the start of the *For Whom the Bell Tolls*, General Goltz gives Jordan orders to blow the bridge when the bombing starts, no sooner. The narrator comments on these orders:

> …and having seen the bridge and worked out and simplified the problem it would have been to surprise the posts and blow it in a normal way, he resented Golz's orders, and the necessity for them. He resented them for what they could do to him and for what they could do to this old man. They were bad orders all right for those who would have to carry them out.
>
> And that is not the way to think, he told himself, and there is not you, and there are no people that things must not happen to. Neither you nor this old man is anything. You are instruments to do your duty.

Jordan is trapped by orders. It is not an error in his judgment that gives him the bogus orders, and therefore he is not a tragic hero. Actually, the character Pablo has more potential as a tragic figure than Jordan; Pablo is a broken man. Jordan is fearful of death but his heroics and his consistent nature defy the tragic mode. Pablo on the other hand, has coldly executed prisoners, and created a murderous and bloody gauntlet-run for the fascist citizens of a town Pablo claimed as his own. Pilar tells of Pablo's organizational skills during the executions pf the fascist townspeople:

> Pablo organized it all as he did the attack on the barracks. First he had the entrances to the streets blocked off with carts as though to organize the plaza for a *capea*. For an amateur bull-fight. The fascists were all held in the Ayuntamiento, the city hall, which was the largest building on one side of the plaza. It was there the clock was set in the wall and it was in the building under the arcade that the club of the fascists was. And under the arcade on the sidewalk in front of their club was where they had their chairs and tables for their club…

Pablo stages the executions like a bullfight but not as a spectator sport—he intends to force the Republicans to murder their fellow citizens, the Fascists. After all the butchering, Pablo falls, as a tragic hero must. He shows remorse for what he has done, even though he acted in a situation of war. Pablo wants to escape from his internal hell, like Oedipus he tries to blind himself—only Pablo uses wine to keep himself from reliving the horrors of his actions. In *The Sun Also Rises* there is a similar reaction to the horror of war—Jake and Brett et al, are trying to drink themselves blind. Of course it doesn't work, but that's what makes for tragic hopelessness in Pablo, Oedipus, and Jake and Brett.

Hemingway's artistic prowess is found in all of his works to some degree. His works often exhibit tragic elements and probe the depths of despair and nothingness. Although the reader can experience good wine, fresh air, and the harmony of the woods, there is a nothingness, what he calls "nada," and emptiness lurking in his writing. Hemingway doesn't project possibilities for the future. He leaves us lingering on all that he has not talked about, the things left unsaid. The Spanish word *nada* means "nothing" in English. In his early work, "A Clean Well-Lighted Place," the author gives us a glimpse into the world of nothing or *nada*. It begins with a description of an old man in a café. Two waiters discuss the old man:

> "Last week he tried to commit suicide," one waiter said.
> "Why?
> "He was in despair."
> "What about?"
> "Nothing."
> "How do you know it was nothing?"
> "He has plenty of money."

With these few words of dialogue, Hemingway will initiate us into the world of nothingness. The author portrays two kinds of people, the kind who have something to go home to and the kind who don't. The older waiter reveals his kinship to the old man, he says, "I am one of those who like to stay late at the café … with all those who do not want to go to bed. With all those who need a light for the night." The older waiter knows the desperation of the old man and Hemingway reveals this to us:

> It was a nothing that he knew too well. It was all a nothing and a man was nothing too. It was only that and light was all it needed and a certain cleanness and order. Some lived in it and never felt it but he knew it all was nada y pues nada y nada y pues nada. Our nada who art in nada, nada be thy name thy kingdom nada thy will be nada in nada as it is in nada. Give us this nada our daily nada and nada us our nada as we nada our nadas and nada us into nada…

The old waiter goes home to the torture of lying in bed, waiting for sleep. He is bothered by the imminent nothingness that encroaches on him. He is only safe from it in a clean, well-lighted place, a clean café perhaps. What is the nothingness? It is the meaninglessness of life, the terror of darkness that brings insomnia. But it is not death; death is the release from nada that the old man seeks by hanging himself. The waiter finally chalks it up to insomnia and says, "Many must have it." He is right of course. Hemingway lets us know that there are many seeking to avoid the questions of desperate nothingness that pervade a human existence dogged by meaningless repetition of chanted prayers, words, and actions. We are all trapped like Brett is, rats running in a wheel, pondering the inescapable query: is this all there is? Hemingway's characters try to deal with the nothingness. In existentialism some people succumb to this void, this nothingness, remaining in a semiconscious state, paralyzed by its vastness. Those lucky few, who experience despair at the absurdity of it all, can experience the possibility of choice and action, thus creating a meaningful existence. Hemingway's powerful works often reveal those who are stuck in the existential mud and can't get out. "A Clean Well-Lighted Place" is like a visit to limbo; even the waiter who wants to go home early may be unpleasantly surprised if he does. In Hemingway the winner takes nothing, because nothingness is all there is. Hemingway's insistent, subversive tone seldom offers a glimpse of hope. It may be that without his direct style, Hemingway could never have congealed such devastating philosophy, so simple, yet so powerful.

EDMUND WILSON

Hemingway: Gauge of Morale

I

Ernest Hemingway's *In Our Time* was an odd and original book. It had the appearance of a miscellany of stories and fragments; but actually the parts hung together and produced a definite effect. There were two distinct series of pieces which alternated with one another: one a set of brief and brutal sketches of police shootings, bullfight crises, hangings of criminals, and incidents of the war; and the other a set of short stories dealing in its principal sequence with the growing-up of an American boy against a landscape of idyllic Michigan, but interspersed also with glimpses of American soldiers returning home. It seems to have been Hemingway's intention—'*In Our Time*'—that the war should set the key for the whole. The cold-bloodedness of the battles and executions strikes a discord with the sensitiveness and candor of the boy at home in the States; and presently the boy turns up in Europe in one of the intermediate vignettes as a soldier in the Italian army, hit in the spine by machine-gun fire and trying to talk to a dying Italian: '*Senta*, Rinaldi. *Senta*,' he says, 'you and me, we've made a separate peace.'

But there is a more fundamental relationship between the pieces of the two series. The shooting of Nick in the war does not really connect two different worlds: has he not found in the butchery abroad the same world that he knew back in Michigan? Was not life in the Michigan woods equally destructive and cruel? He had gone once with his father, the doctor, when he had performed a Caesarean operation on an Indian squaw with a jackknife and no anaesthetic and had sewed her up with fishing leaders, while the Indian hadn't been able to bear it and had cut his throat in his bunk. Another time, when the doctor had saved the life of a squaw, her Indian had picked a quarrel with him rather than pay him in work. And Nick himself had sent his girl about her business when he had found out how terrible her mother was. Even fishing in Big Two-Hearted River—away and free in the woods—he had been conscious in a curious way of the cruelty inflicted on the fish, even of the silent agonies endured by the live bait, the grasshoppers kicking on the hook.

Not that life isn't enjoyable. Talking and drinking with one's friends is great fun; fishing in Big Two-Hearted River is a tranquil exhilaration. But the brutality of life is always there, and it is somehow bound up with the enjoyment. Bullfights are especially enjoyable. It is even exhilarating to build a simply priceless barricade and pot the enemy as they are trying to get over it. The condition of life is pain; and the joys of the most innocent surface are somehow tied to its stifled pangs.

The resolution of this dissonance in art made the beauty of Hemingway's stories. He had in the process tuned a marvelous prose. Out of the colloquial American speech, with its simple declarative sentences and its strings of Nordic monosyllables, he got effects of the utmost subtlety. F. M. Ford has found the perfect simile for the impression produced by this writing: 'Hemingway's words strike you, each one, as if they were pebbles sketched fresh from a brook. They live and shine, each in its place. So one of his pages has the effect of a brook-bottom into which you look down through the flowing water. The words form a tesellation, each in order beside the other.'

Looking back, we can see how this style was already being refined and developed at a time—fifty years before—when it was regarded in most literary quarters as hopelessly non-literary and vulgar. Had there not been the nineteenth chapter of *Huckleberry Finn*?—'Two or three nights went by; I reckon—I might say they swum by; they slid along so quick and smooth and lovely. Here is the way we put in the time. It was a monstrous big river down there—sometimes a mile and a half wide,' and so forth. These pages, when we happen to meet them in Carl Van Doren's anthology of world literature, stand up in a striking way beside a passage of description from Turgenev; and the pages which Hemingway was later to write about American wood and water are equivalents to the transcriptions by Turgenev—the *Sportsman's*

Notebook is much admired by Hemingway—of Russian forests and fields. Each has brought to an immense and wild country the freshness of a new speech and a sensibility not yet conventionalized by literary associations. Yet it *is* the European sensibility which has come to Big Two-Hearted River, where the Indians are now obsolescent; in those solitudes it feels for the first time the cold current, the hot morning sun, sees the pine stumps, smells the sweet fern. And along with the mottled trout, with its 'clear water-over-gravel color,' the boy from the American Middle West fishes up a nice little masterpiece.

In the meantime there had been also Ring Lardner, Sherwood Anderson, Gertrude Stein, using this American language for irony, lyric poetry or psychological insight. Hemingway seems to have learned from them all. But he is now able to charge this naïve accent with a new complexity of emotion, a new shade of emotion: a malaise. The wholesale shattering of human beings in which he has taken part has given the boy a touch of panic.

II

The next fishing trip is strikingly different. Perhaps the first had been an idealization. It is possible to attain to such sensuous bliss merely through going alone into the woods: smoking, fishing, and eating, with no thought about anyone else or about anything one has ever done or will ever be obliged to do? At any rate, today, in *The Sun Also Rises*, all the things that are wrong with human life are there on the holiday, too—though one tries to keep them back out of the foreground and to occupy one's mind with the trout, caught now in a stream of the Pyrenees, and with the kidding of the friend from the States. The feeling of insecurity has deepened. The young American now appears in a seriously damaged condition: he has somehow been incapacitated sexually through wounds received in the war. He is in love with one of those international sirens who flourished in the cafés of the post-war period and whose ruthless and uncontrollable infidelities, in such a circle as that depicted by Hemingway, have made any sort of security impossible for the relations between women and men. The lovers of such a woman turn upon and rend one another because they are powerless to make themselves felt by *her*.

The casualties of the bullfight at Pamplona, to which these young people have gone for the *fiesta*, only reflect the blows and betrayals of demoralized human beings out of hand. What is the tiresome lover with whom the lady has just been off on a casual escapade, and who is unable to understand that he has been discarded, but the man who, on his way to the bull ring, has been accidentally gored by the bull? The young American who tells the story is the only character who keeps up standards of conduct, and he is prevented by his disability from dominating and directing the woman, who otherwise, it is intimated, might love him. Here the membrane of the style has been stretched taut to convey the vibrations of these qualms. The dry sunlight and the green summer landscapes have been invested with a sinister quality which must be new in literature. One enjoys the sun and the green as one enjoys suckling pigs and Spanish wine, but the uneasiness and apprehension are undruggable.

Yet one can catch hold of a code in all the drunkenness and the social chaos. 'Perhaps as you went along you did learn something,' Jake, the hero reflects at one point. 'I did not care what it was all about. All I wanted to know was how to live in it. Maybe if you found out how to live in it, you learned from that what it was all about.' 'Everybody behaves badly. Give them the proper chance,' he says later to Lady Brett.

'"You wouldn't behave badly." Brett looked at me.' In the end, she sends for Jake, who finds her alone in a hotel. She has left her regular lover for a young bullfighter, and this boy has for the first time inspired her with a respect which has restrained her from 'ruining' him: 'You know it makes one feel rather good deciding not to be a bitch.' We suffer and we make suffer, and everybody loses out in the long run; but in the meantime one can lose with honor.

This code still markedly figures, still supplies a dependable moral backbone, in Hemingway's next book of short stories, *Men Without Women*. Here Hemingway has mastered his method of economy in apparent casualness and relevance in apparent indirection, and has turned his sense of what happens and the way in which it happens into something as hard and clear as a crystal but as disturbing as a great lyric. Yet it is usually some principle of courage, of honor, of pity—that is, some principle of sportsmanship in its largest human sense—upon which the drama hinges. The old bullfighter in *The Undefeated* is defeated in everything except the spirit which will not accept defeat. You get the bull or he gets you: if you die, you can die game; there are certain things you cannot do. The burlesque show manager in *A Pursuit Race* refrains from waking his advance publicity agent when he overtakes him and realizes that the man has just lost a long struggle against whatever anguish it is that has driven him to drink and dope. 'They got a cure for that,' the manager had said to him before he went to sleep; '"No," William Campbell said, "they haven't got a cure for anything."' The burned major in *A Simple Enquiry*—that strange picture of the bedrock stoicism compatible with the abasement of war—has the decency not to dismiss the orderly who has rejected his proposition. The brutalized Alpine peasant who has been in the habit of hanging a lantern on the jaws of the stiffened corpse of his wife, stood in the corner of the woodshed till the spring will make it possible to bury her, is ashamed to drink with the sexton after the latter has found out what he has done. And there is a little sketch of Roman soldiers just after the Crucifixion: 'You see me slip the old spear into him?—You'll get into trouble doing that some day.—It was the least I could do for him. I'll tell you he looked pretty good to me in there today.'

This Hemingway of the middle twenties—*The Sun Also Rises* came out in '26—expressed the romantic disillusion and set the favorite pose for the period. It was the moment of gallantry in heartbreak, grim and nonchalant banter, and heroic dissipation. The great watchword was 'Have a drink'; and in the bars of New York and Paris the young people were getting to talk like Hemingway.

III

The novel, *A Farewell to Arms*, which followed *Men Without Women*, is in a sense not so serious an affair. Beautifully written and quite moving of course it is. Probably no other book has caught so well the strangeness of life in the army for an American in Europe during the war. The new places to which one was sent of which one had never heard, and the things that turned out to be in them; the ordinary people of foreign countries as one saw them when one was quartered among them or obliged to perform some common work with them; the pleasures of which one managed to cheat the war, intensified by the uncertainty and horror—and the uncertainty, nevertheless, almost become a constant, the horror almost taken for granted; the love affairs, always subject to being suddenly broken up and yet carried on while they lasted in a spirit of irresponsible freedom which derived from one's having forfeited control of all one's other actions—this Hemingway got into his book, written long enough after the events for them to present themselves under an aspect fully idyllic.

But *A Farewell to Arms* is a tragedy, and the lovers are shown as innocent victims with no relation to the forces that torment them. They themselves are not tormented within by that dissonance between personal satisfaction and the suffering one shares with others which it has been Hemingway's triumph to handle. *A Farewell to Arms*, as the author once said, is a *Romeo and Juliet*. And when Catherine and her lover emerge from the stream of action—the account of the Caporetto retreat is Hemingway's best sustained piece of narrative—when they escape from the alien necessities of which their romance has been merely an accident, which have been writing their story for them, then we see that they are not in themselves convincing as human personalities. And we are confronted with the paradox that Hemingway, who possesses so remarkable a mimetic gift in getting the tone of social and national types and in making his people talk appropriately, has not shown any very solid sense of character, or, indeed, any real interest in it. The people in his short stories are satisfactory because he has only to hit them off: the point of the story does not lie in personalities, but in the emotion to which a situation gives rise. This is true even in *The Sun Also Rises*, where the characters are sketched with wonderful cleverness. But in *A Farewell to Arms*, as soon as we are brought into real intimacy with the lovers, as soon as the author is obliged to see them through a searching personal experience, we find merely an idealized relationship, the abstractions of a lyric emotion.

With *Death in the Afternoon*, three years later, a new development for Hemingway commences. He writes a book not merely in the first person, but in the first person in his own character as Hemingway, and the results are unexpected and disconcerting. *Death in the Afternoon* has its value as an exposition of bullfighting; and Hemingway is able to use the subject as a text for an explicit statement of his conception of man eternally pitting himself— he thinks the bullfight a ritual of this—against animal force and the odds of death. But the book is partly infected by a queer kind of maudlin emotion, which sounds at once neurotic and drunken. He overdoes his glorification of the bravery and martyrdom of the bullfighter. No doubt the professional expert at risking his life single-handed is impressive in contrast to the flatness and unreality of much of the business of the modern world; but this admirable miniaturist in prose has already made the point perhaps more tellingly in the little prose poem called *Banal Story*. Now he offsets the virility of the bullfighters by anecdotes of the male homosexuals that frequent the Paris cafés, at the same time that he puts his chief celebration of the voluptuous excitement of the spectacle into the mouth of an imaginary old lady. The whole thing becomes a little hysterical.

The master of that precise and clean style now indulges in purple patches which go on spreading for pages. I am not one of those who admire the last chapter of *Death in the Afternoon*, with its rich, all too rich, unrollings of memories of good times in Spain, and with its what seem to me irrelevant reminiscences of the soliloquy of Mrs. Bloom in *Ulysses*. Also, there are interludes of kidding of a kind which Hemingway handles with skill when he assigns them to characters in his stories, but in connection with which he seems to become incapable of exercising good sense or good taste as soon as he undertakes them in his own person (the burlesque *Torrents of Spring* was an early omen of this). In short, we are compelled to recognize that, as soon as Hemingway drops the burning-glass of the disciplined and objective art with which he has learned to concentrate in a story the light of the emotions that flood in on him, he straightway becomes befuddled, slops over.

This befuddlement is later to go further, but in the meantime he publishes another volume of stories—*Winner Take Nothing*—which is almost up to its predecessor. In this collection he deals much more effectively than in *Death in the Afternoon* with that theme of contemporary decadence which is implied in his panegyric of the bullfighter. The first of these stories, *After the Storm*, is another of his variations—and one of the finest—on the theme of keeping up a code of decency among the hazards and pains of life. A fisherman goes out to plunder a wreck: he dives down to break in through a porthole, but inside he sees a woman with rings on her hands and her hair floating loose in the water, and he thinks about the passengers and crew being suddenly plunged to their deaths (he has almost been killed himself in a drunken fight the night before). He sees the cloud of sea birds screaming around, and he finds that he is unable to break the glass with his wrench and that he loses the anchor grapple with which he next tries to attack it. So he finally goes away and leaves the job to the Greeks, who blow the boat open and clean her out.

But in general the emotions of insecurity here obtrude themselves and dominate the book. Two of the stories deal with the hysteria of soldiers falling off the brink of their nerves under the strain of the experiences of the war, which here no longer presents an idyllic aspect; another deals with a group of patients in a hospital, at the same time crippled and hopeless; still another (a five-page masterpiece) with a waiter, who, both on his own and on his customers' account, is reluctant to go home at night, because he feels the importance of a 'clean well-lighted cafe' as a refuge from the 'nothing' that people fear. *God Rest You Merry Gentlemen* repeats the theme of castration of *The Sun Also Rises*; and four of the stories are concerned more or less with male or female homosexuality. In the last story, *Fathers and Sons*, Hemingway reverts to the Michigan woods, as if to take the curse off the rest: young Nick had once enjoyed a nice Indian girl with plump legs and hard little breasts on the needles of the hemlock woods.

These stories and the interludes in *Death in the Afternoon* must have been written during the years that followed the stock-market crash. They are full of the apprehension of losing control of oneself which is aroused by the getting out of hand of a social-economic system, as well as of the fear of impotence which seems to accompany the loss of social mastery. And there is in such a story as *A Clean Well-Lighted Place* the feeling of having got to the end of everything, of having given up heroic attitudes and wanting only the illusion of peace.

IV

And now, in proportion as the characters in his stories run out of fortitude and bravado, he passes into a phase where he is occupied with building up his public personality. He has already now become a legend, as Mencken was in the twenties; he is the Hemingway of the handsome photographs with the sportsman's tan and the outdoor grin, with the ominous resemblance to Clark Gable, who poses with giant marlin which he has just hauled in off Key West. And unluckily—but for an American inevitably—the opportunity soon presents itself to exploit this personality for profit: he turns up delivering Hemingway monologues in well-paying and trashy magazines; and the Hemingway of these loose disquisitions, arrogant, belligerent and boastful, is certainly the worst-invented character to be found in the author's work. If he is obnoxious, the effect is somewhat mitigated by the fact that he is intrinsically incredible.

There would be no point in mentioning this journalism at all, if it did not seem somewhat to have contributed to the writing of certain unsatisfactory books. *Green Hills of Africa* (1935) owes its failure to falling between the two *genres* of personal exhibitionism and fiction. 'The writer has attempted,' says Hemingway, 'to write an absolutely true book to see whether the shape of a country and the pattern of a month's action can, if truly presented, compete with a work of the imagination.' He does try to present his own rôle objectively, and there is a genuine Hemingway theme—the connection between success at big-game hunting and sexual self-respect—involved in his adventures as he presents them. But the sophisticated technique of the fiction writer comes to look artificial when it is applied to a series of real happenings; and the necessity of sticking to what really happened makes impossible the typical characters and incidents which give point to a work of fiction. The monologues by the false, the publicity, Hemingway with which the narrative is interspersed are almost as bad as the ones that he has been writing for the magazines. He inveighs with much scorn against the literary life and against the professional literary man of the cities; and then manages to give the impression that he himself is a professional literary man of the touchiest and most self-conscious kind. He delivers a self-confident lecture on the high possibilities of prose writing; and then produces such a sentence as the following: 'Going downhill steeply made these Spanish shooting boots too short in the toe and there was an old argument, about this length of boot and whether the bootmaker, whose part I had taken, unwittingly first, only as interpreter, and finally embraced his theory patriotically as a whole and, I believed, by logic, had overcome it by adding onto the heel.' As soon as Hemingway begins speaking in the first person, he seems to lose his bearings, not merely as a critic of life, but even as a craftsman.

In another and significant way, *Green Hills of Africa* is disappointing. *Death in the Afternoon* did provide a lot of data on bullfighting and build up for us the bullfighting world; but its successor tells us little about Africa. Hemingway keeps affirming—as if in accents of defiance against those who would engage his attention for social problems—his passionate enthusiasm for the African country and his perfect satisfaction with the hunter's life; but he has produced what must be one of the only books ever written which make Africa and its animals seem dull. Almost the only thing we learn about the animals is that Hemingway wants to kill them. And as for the natives, though there is one fine description of a tribe of marvelous trained runners, the principle impression we get of them is that they were simple and inferior people who enormously admired Hemingway.

It is not only that, as his critics of the Left had been complaining, he shows no interest in political issues, but that his interest in his fellow beings seems actually to be drying up. It is as if he were throwing himself on African hunting as something to live for and believe in, as something through which to realize himself; and as if, expecting of it too much, he had got out of it abnormally little, less than he is willing to admit. The disquiet of the Hemingway of the twenties had been, as I have said, undruggable—that is, in his books themselves, he had tried to express it, not drug it, had given it an appeasement in art; but now there sets in, in the Hemingway of the thirties, what seems to be a deliberate self-drugging. The situation is indicated objectively in *The Gambler, the Nun and the Radio*, one of the short stories of 1933, in which everything from daily bread to 'a belief in any new form of government' is characterized as 'the opium of the people' by an empty-hearted patient in a hospital.

But at last there did rush into this vacuum the blast of the social issue, which had been roaring in the wind like a forest fire.

Out of a series of short stories that Hemingway had written about a Florida waterside character he decided to make a little epic. The result was *To Have and Have Not*, which seems to me the poorest of all his stories. Certainly some deep agitation is working upon Hemingway the artist. Craftsmanship and style, taste and sense, have all alike gone by the board. The negative attitude toward human beings has here become definitely malignant: the hero is like a wooden-headed Punch, always knocking people on the head (inferiors—Chinamen or Cubans); or, rather, he combines the characteristics of Punch with those of Popeye the Sailor in the animated cartoon in the movies. As the climax to a series of prodigies, this stupendous pirate-smuggler named Harry Morgan succeeds, alone, unarmed, and with only a hook for one hand—though at the cost of a mortal wound—in outwitting and destroying with their own weapons four men carrying revolvers and a machine gun, by whom he has been shanghaied in a launch. The only way in which Hemingway's outlaw suffers by comparison with Popeye is that his creator has not tried to make him plausible by explaining that he does it all on spinach.

The impotence of a decadent society has here been exploited deliberately, but less successfully than in the earlier short stories. Against a background of homosexuality, impotence and masturbation among the wealthy holiday-makers in Florida, Popeye-Morgan is shown gratifying his wife with the same indefatigable dexterity which he has displayed in his other feats; and there is a choral refrain of praise of his *cojones*, which wells up in the last pages of the book when the abandoned Mrs. Popeye regurgitates Molly Bloom's soliloquy.

To be a man in such a world of maggots is noble, but it is not enough. Besides the maggots, there are double-crossing rats, who will get you if they are given the slightest chance. What is most valid in *To Have and Have Not* is the idea—conveyed better, perhaps, in the first of the series of episodes than in the final scenes of massacre and agony—that in an atmosphere (here revolutionary Cuba) in which man has been set against man, in which it is always a question whether your companion is not preparing to cut your throat, the most sturdy and straightforward American will turn suspicious and cruel. Harry Morgan is made to realize as he dies that to fight this bad world alone is hopeless. Again Hemingway, with his barometric accuracy, has rendered a moral atmosphere that was prevalent at the moment he was writing—a moment when social relations were subjected to severe tensions, when they seemed sometimes already disintegrating. But the heroic Hemingway legend has at this point invaded his fiction and, inflaming and inflating his symbols, has produced an implausible hybrid, half Hemingway character, half nature myth.

Hemingway had not himself particularly labored this moral of individualism *versus* solidarity, but the critics of the Left labored it for him and received his least creditable piece of fiction as the delivery of a new revelation. The progress of the Communist faith among our writers since the beginning of the depression has followed a peculiar course. That the aims and beliefs of Marx and Lenin should have come through to the minds of intellectuals who had been educated in the bourgeois tradition as great awakeners of conscience, a great light, was quite natural and entirely desirable. But the conception of the dynamic Marxist will, the exaltation of the Marxist religion, seized the members of the professional classes like a capricious contagion or hurricane, which shakes one and leaves his neighbor standing, then returns to lay hold on the second after the first has become quiet again. In the moment of seizure, each one of them saw a scroll unrolled from the heavens, on which Marx and Lenin and Stalin, the Bolsheviks of 1917, the Soviets of the Five-Year Plan, and the GPU of the Moscow trials were all a part of the same great purpose. Later the convert, if he were capable of it, would get over his first phase of snow blindness and learn to see real people and conditions, would study the development of Marxism in terms of nations, periods, personalities, instead of logical deductions from abstract propositions or—as in the case of the more naïve or dishonest—of simple incantatory slogans. But for many there was at least a moment when the key to all the mysteries of human history seemed suddenly to have been placed in their hands, when an infallible guide to thought and behavior seemed to have been given them in a few easy formulas.

Hemingway was hit pretty late. He was still in *Death in the Afternoon* telling the 'world-savers,' sensibly enough, that they should 'get to see' the world 'clear and as a whole. Then any part you make will represent the whole, if it's made truly. The thing to do is work and learn to make it.' Later he jibed at the literary radicals, who talked but couldn't take it; and one finds even in *To Have and Have Not* a crack about a 'highly paid Hollywood director, whose brain is in the process of outlasting his liver so that he will end up calling himself a Communist, to save his soul.' Then the challenge of the fight itself—Hemingway never could resist a physical challenge—the natural impulse to dedicate oneself to something bigger than big-game hunting and bullfighting, and the fact that the class war had broken out in a country to which he was romantically attached, seem to have combined to make him align himself with the Communists as well as the Spanish Loyalists at a time when the Marxist philosophy had been pretty completely shelved by the Kremlin, now reactionary as well as corrupt, and when the Russians were lending the Loyalists only help enough to preserve, as they imagined would be possible, the balance of power against Fascism while they acted at the same time as a police force to beat down the real social revolution.

Hemingway raised money for the Loyalists, reported the battle fronts. He even went so far as to make a speech at a congress of the League of American Writers, an organization rigged by the supporters of the Stalinist régime in Russia and full of precisely the type of literary revolutionists that he had been ridiculing a little while before. Soon the Stalinists had taken him in tow, and he was feverishly denouncing as Fascists other writers who criticized the Kremlin. It has been one of the expedients of the Stalin administration in maintaining its power and covering up its crimes to condemn on trumped-up charges of Fascist conspiracy, and even to kidnap and murder, its political opponents of the left; and, along with the food and munitions, the Russians had brought to the war in Spain what the Austrian journalist Willi Schlamm called that diversion of doubtful value for the working class: 'Herr Vyshinsky's Grand Guignol.'

The result of this was a play, *The Fifth Column*, which, though it is good reading for the way the characters talk, is an exceedingly silly production. The hero, though an Anglo-American, is an agent of the Communist secret police, engaged in catching Fascist spies in Spain; and his principle exploit in the course of the play is clearing out, with the aid of a single Communist, an artillery post manned by seven Fascists. The scene is like a pushover and getaway from one of the cruder Hollywood Westerns. It is in the nature of a small boy's fantasy, and would probably be considered extravagant by most writers of books for boys.

The tendency on Hemingway's part to indulge himself in these boyish day-dreams seems to begin to get the better of his realism at the end of *A Farewell to Arms*, where the hero, after many adventures of fighting, escaping, love-making and drinking, rows his lady thirty-five kilometers on a cold and rainy night; and we have seen what it could do for Harry Morgan. Now, as if with the conviction that the cause and the efficiency of the GPU have added several cubits to his stature, he has let this tendency loose; and he has also found in the GPU's grim duty a pretext to give rein to the appetite for describing scenes of killing which has always been a feature of his work. He has progressed from grasshoppers and trout through bulls and lions and kudus to Chinamen and Cubans, and now to Fascists. Hitherto the act of destruction has given rise for him to complex emotions: he has indentified himself not merely with the injurer but also with the injured; there has been a masochistic complement to the sadism. But now this paradox which splits our natures, and which has instigated some of Hemingway's best stories, need no longer present perplexities to his mind. The Fascists are dirty bastards, and to kill them is a righteous act. He who had made a separate peace, who had said farewell to arms, has found a reason for taking them up again in a spirit of rabietic fury unpleasantly reminiscent of the spy mania and the sacred anti-German rage which took possession of so many civilians and staff officers under the stimulus of the last war.

Not that the compensatory trauma of the typical Hemingway protagonist is totally absent even here. The main episode is the hero's brief love affair and voluntary breaking off with a beautiful and adoring girl whose acquaintance he has made in Spain. As a member of the Junior League and a graduate of Vassar, she represents for him—it seems a little hard on her—that leisure-class playworld from which he is trying to get away. But in view of the fact that from the very first scenes he treats her with more or less open contempt, the action is rather lacking in suspense as the sacrifice is rather feeble in moral value. One takes no stock at all in the intimation that Mr. Philip may later be sent to mortify himself in a camp for training Young Pioneers. And in the meantime he has fun killing Fascists.

In *The Fifth Column*, the drugging process has been carried further still: the hero, who has become finally indistinguishable from the false or publicity Hemingway, has here dosed himself not only with whiskey, but with a seductive and desirous woman, for whom he has the most admirable reasons for not taking any responsibility, with sacred rage, with the excitement of a bombardment, and with the indulgence in that headiest of sports, for which he has now the same excellent reasons: the bagging of human beings.

V

You may fear, after reading *The Fifth Column*, that Hemingway will never sober up; but as you go on to his short stories of this period, you find that your apprehensions were unfounded. Three of these stories have a great deal more body—they are longer and more complex—than the comparatively meager anecdotes collected in *Winner Take Nothing*. And here are his real artistic successes with the material of his adventures in Africa, which make up for the miscarried *Green Hills: The Short Happy Life of Francis Macomber* and *The Snows of Kilimanjaro*, which disengage, by dramatizing them objectively, the themes he had attempted in the earlier book but that had never really got themselves presented. And here is at least a beginning of a real artistic utilization of Hemingway's experience in Spain: an incident of the war in two pages which outweighs the whole of *The Fifth Column* and all his Spanish dispatches, a glimpse of an old man, 'without politics,' who has so far occupied his life in taking care of eight pigeons, two goats and a cat, but who has now been dislodged and separated from his pets by the advance of the Fascist armies. It is a story which takes its place among the war prints of Callot and Goya, artists whose union of elegance with sharpness has already been recalled by Hemingway in his earlier battle pieces: a story which might have been written about almost any war.

And here—what is very remarkable—is a story, *The Capital of the World*, which finds an objective symbol for, precisely, what is wrong with *The Fifth*

Column. A young boy who has come up from the country and waits on table in a pension in Madrid gets accidentally stabbed with a meat knife while playing at bullfighting with the dishwasher. This is the simple anecdote, but Hemingway has built in behind it all the life of the pension and the city: the priesthood, the working-class movement, the grown-up bullfighters who have broken down or missed out. 'The boy Paco,' Hemingway concludes, 'had never known about any of this nor about what all these people would be doing on the next day and on other days to come. He had no idea how they really lived nor how they ended. He did not realize they ended. He died, as the Spanish phrase has it, full of illusions. He had not had time in his life to lose any of them, or even, at the end, to complete an act of contrition.' So he registers in this very fine piece the discrepancy between the fantasies of boyhood and the realities of the grown-up world. Hemingway the artist, who feels things truly and cannot help recording what he feels, has actually said good-bye to these fantasies at a time when the war correspondent is making himself ridiculous by attempting to hang on to them still.

The emotion which principally comes through in *Francis Macomber* and *The Snows of Kilimanjaro*—as it figures also in *The Fifth Column*—is a growing antagonism to women. Looking back, one can see at this point that the tendency has been there all along. In *The Doctor and the Doctor's Wife*, the boy Nick goes out squirrel-hunting with his father instead of obeying the summons of his mother; in *Cross Country Snow*, he regretfully says farewell to male companionship on a skiing expedition in Switzerland, when he is obliged to go back to the States so that his wife can have her baby. The young man in *Hills Like White Elephants* compels his girl to have an abortion contrary to her wish; another story, *A Canary for One*, bites almost unbearably but exquisitely on the loneliness to be endured by a wife after she and her husband shall have separated; the peasant of *An Alpine Idyll* abuses the corpse of his wife (these last three appear under the general title *Men Without Women*). Brett in *The Sun Also Rises* is an exclusively destructive force: she might be a better woman if she were mated with Jake, the American; but actually he is protected against her and is in a sense revenging his own sex through being unable to do anything for her sexually. Even the hero of *A Farewell to Arms* eventually destroys Catherine—after enjoying her abject devotion—by giving her a baby, itself born dead. The only women with whom Nick Adams' relations are perfectly satisfactory are the little Indian girls of his boyhood who are in a position of hopeless social disadvantage and have no power over the behavior of the white male—so that he can get rid of them the moment he has done with them. Thus in *The Fifth Column* Mr. Philip brutally breaks off with Dorothy—he has been rescued from her demoralizing influence by his enlistment in the

Communist crusade, just as the hero of *The Sun Also Rises* has been saved by his physical disability—to revert to a little Moorish whore. Even Harry Morgan, who is represented as satisfying his wife on the scale of a Paul Bunyan, deserts her in the end by dying and leaves her racked by the cruelest desire.

And now this instinct to get the woman down presents itself frankly as a fear that the woman will get the man down. The men in both these African stories are married to American bitches of the most soul-destroying sort. The hero of *The Snows of Kilimanjaro* loses his soul and dies of futility on a hunting expedition in Africa, out of which he has failed to get what he had hoped. The story is not quite stripped clean of the trashy moral attitudes which have been coming to disfigure the author's work: the hero, a seriously intentioned and apparently promising writer, goes on a little sloppily over the dear early days in Paris when he was earnest, happy and poor, and blames a little hysterically the rich woman whom he has married and who has debased him. Yet it is one of Hemingway's remarkable stories. There is a wonderful piece of writing at the end when the reader is made to realize that what has seemed to be an escape by plane, with the sick man looking down on Africa, is only the dream of a dying man. The other story, *Francis Macomber*, perfectly realizes its purpose. Here the male saves his soul at the last minute, and then is actually shot down by his woman, who does not want him to have a soul. Here Hemingway has at last got what Thurber calls the war between men and women right out into the open and has written a terrific fable on the impossible civilized woman who despises the civilized man for his failure in initiative and nerve and then jealously tries to break him down as soon as he begins to exhibit any. (It ought to be noted, also, that whereas in *Green Hills of Africa* the descriptions tended to weigh down the narrative with their excessive circumstantiality, the landscapes and animals of *Francis Macomber* are alive and unfalteringly proportioned.)

Going back over Hemingway's books today, we can see clearly what an error of the politicos it was to accuse him of an indifference to society. His whole work is a criticism of society: he has responded to every pressure of the moral atmosphere of the time, as it is felt at the roots of human relations, with a sensitivity almost unrivaled. Even his preoccupation with licking the gang in the next block and being known as the best basketball player in high school has its meaning in the present epoch. After all, whatever is done in the world, political as well as athletic, depends on personal courage and strength. With Hemingway, courage and strength are always thought of in physical terms, so that he tends to give an impression that the bullfighter who can take it and dish it out is more of a man than any other kind of man, and that the sole duty of the revolutionary socialist is to get the counter-revolutionary gang before they get him.

But ideas, however correct, will never prevail by themselves: there must be people who are prepared to stand or fall with them, and the ability to act on principle is still subject to the same competitive laws which operate in sporting contests and sexual relations. Hemingway has expressed with genius the terrors of the modern man at the danger of losing control of his world, and he has also, within his scope, provided his own kind of antidote. This antidote, paradoxically, is almost entirely moral. Despite Hemingway's preoccupation with physical contests, his heroes are almost always defeated physically, nervously, practically: their victories are moral ones. He himself, when he trained himself stubbornly on his unconventional unmarketable art in a Paris which had other fashions, gave the prime example of such a victory; and if he has sometimes, under the menace of the general panic, seemed on the point of going to pieces as an artist, he has always pulled himself together the next moment. The principle of the Bourdon gauge, which is used to measure the pressure of liquids, is that a tube which has been curved into a coil will tend to straighten out in proportion as the liquid inside it is subjected to an increasing pressure.

The appearance of *For Whom the Bell Tolls* since this essay was written in 1939 carries the straightening process further. Here Hemingway has largely sloughed off his Stalinism and has reverted to seeing events in terms of individuals pitted against specific odds. His hero, an American teacher of Spanish who has enlisted on the side of the Loyalists, gives his life to what he regards as the cause of human liberation; but he is frustrated in the task that has been assigned him by the confusion of forces at cross-purposes that are throttling the Loyalist campaign. By the time that he comes to die, he has little to sustain him but the memory of his grandfather's record as a soldier in the American Civil War. The psychology of this young man is presented with a certain sobriety and detachment in comparison with Hemingway's other full-length heroes; and the author has here succeeded as in none of his earlier books in externalizing in plausible characters the elements of his own complex personality. With all this, there is an historical point of view which he has learned from his political adventures: he has aimed to reflect in this episode the whole course of the Spanish War and the tangle of tendencies involved in it.

The weaknesses of the book are its diffuseness—a shape that lacks the concision of his short stories, that sometimes sags and sometimes bulges; and a sort of exploitation of the material, an infusion of the operatic, that lends itself all too readily to the movies.

LIONEL TRILLING

An American in Spain

To anyone at all interested in its author's career—and who is not?—*For Whom the Bell Tolls* will first give a literary emotion. For here, we feel at once, is a restored Hemingway writing to the top of his bent. He does not, as in the period of *To Have and Have Not* and *The Fifth Column*, warp or impede his notable talent with the belief that art is to be used like the automatic rifle. He does not substitute political will for literary insight nor arrogantly pass off his personal rage as social responsibility. Not that his present political attitude is coherent or illuminating; indeed, it is so little of either that it acts as the anarchic element in a work whose total effect is less impressive than many of its parts. Yet at least it is flexible enough, or ambiguous enough, to allow Hemingway a more varied notion of life than he has ever before achieved.

With the themes that bring out his craft most happily Hemingway has never been so good—no one else can make so memorable the events of physical experience, how things look and move and are related to each other. From the beginning of the novel to the end, one has the happy sense of the author's unremitting and successful poetic effort. So great is this effort, indeed, that one is inclined to feel that it is at times even too great, that it becomes conscious of itself almost to priggishness and quite to virtuosity. About some of the very good moments—they are by now famous—one has the uneasy sense that they are rather too obviously "performances": I mean

Lionel Trilling, "An American in Spain," The Partisan Reader, eds., William Phillips and Philip Rahv (New York: Dial Press, Inc., 1946), pp. 639–644. Reprinted by permission of the author.

moments so admirable as the account of the massacre of the fascists by the republicans, as well as moments so much less good because so frankly gaudy as the description of the "smell of death"—the really superlative passages, such as the episode of El Sordo on his hill or Andres making his way through the republican lines, which are equal to Tolstoy in his best battle-manner, are more modestly handled. And the sense of the writer doing his duty up to and beyond the point of supererogation is forced on us in the frequent occurrence of the kind of [**639/640**] prose of which Hemingway has always allowed himself a small, perhaps forgivable, amount when he wishes to deal with emotions which he considers especially difficult, delicate, or noble. This kind of writing, obtrusively "literary," oddly "feminine," is most frequently used for the emotions of love and it is always in as false and fancy taste as this:

> Now as they lay all that before had been shielded was unshielded. Where there had been roughness of fabric all was smooth with a smoothness and firm rounded pressing and a long warm coolness, cool outside and warm within, long and light and closely holding, closely held, lonely, hollow-making with contours, happy-making, young and loving and now all warmly smooth with a hollowing, chest-aching, tight-held loneliness that was such that Robert Jordan felt he could stand it....

Yet the virtuosity and the lapses of taste are but excesses of an effort which is, on the whole, remarkably successful. And if we cannot help thinking a little wryly about how much tragic defeat, how much limitation of political hope, was necessary before Hemingway could be weaned from the novel of arrogant political will, neither can we help being impressed by what he has accomplished in the change.

I speak first and at some length of the style of *For Whom the Bell Tolls* because it seems to me that the power and charm of the book arise almost entirely from the success of the style—from the success of many incidents handled to the full of their possible interest. The power and charm do not arise from the plan of the book as a whole; when the reading is behind us, what we remember is a series of brilliant scenes and a sense of having been almost constantly excited, but we do not remember a general significance. Yet Hemingway, we may be sure, intended that the star-crossed love and heroic death of Robert Jordan should be a real tragedy, a moral and political tragedy which would suggest and embody the tragedy of the Spanish war. In this intention he quite fails. The clue to the failure is the essential inner dullness of his hero. Robert Jordan does not have within himself what alone could have made tragedy out of this remarkable melodrama—he does not in himself embody the tensions which were in the historical events he lived through. His fate is determined by the moral and political contradictions of the historical situation, but he himself explicitly refuses to recognize these contradictions, he stands apart from them. And since it is Jordan's fate that must provide whatever intellectual architectonic the novel is to have, the novel itself [640/641] fails, not absolutely but relatively to its possibility and to its implied intention.

This failure illustrates as well as anything could the point of Philip Rahv's essay, "The Cult of Experience in American Writing" (*Partisan Review*, November-December 1940). For here again we have the imbalance which Mr. Rahv speaks of as characteristic of the American novel—on the one hand the remarkable perception of sensory and emotional fact, on the other hand an inadequacy of intellectual vitality. Consider as an illuminating detail the relation which Hemingway establishes between Robert Jordan and the leaders he admires, Goltz the general and Karkov the journalist. Both are cynical and exceptionally competent men, wholly capable of understanding all the meanings of the revolutionary scene. But they are Europeans and Robert Jordan is not; like the hero of Henry James's *The American*, he knows that there are machinations going on around him, very wrong but very wonderful, which he will never be able to understand. Nor does he really want to understand as his friends do. He wants, he says, to keep his mind in suspension until the war is won. He wants only to feel emotions and ideals, or, as a technician and a brave man, to *do* what he is told. The thinking is for others. Yet, like a Henry James character again, he must penetrate the complex secret; but he has no wish to use it, only to *experience* it, for he likes, as he says, the feeling of being an "insider," which is what one becomes by losing one's American "chastity of mind," telling political lies with the Russians in Gaylord's Hotel.

Hemingway himself, it would seem, has a full awareness of the complex actuality of the situation. Again and again, and always pungently, he brings to our notice the tensions and contradictions of a revolutionary civil war—describes the cynicism and intrigue and shabby vice of the Russian politicos, pointedly questions the political virtue of La Pasionaria, paints André Marty, in a brilliant and terrifying scene, as a homicidal psychopath under the protection of the Comintern, speaks out about the sins of Loyalist leaders and has only a small and uncertain inclination to extenuate the special sins of the Communists. Indeed, there is scarcely a charge that anti-Stalinists might have made during the war whose truth Hemingway does not in one way or another avow. Yet by some failure of mind or of seriousness, he cannot permit these political facts to become integral with the book by entering importantly into the mind of the hero. Robert Jordan, to be sure, thinks a good deal about all these things, but almost always as if they were not much more than—to use the [641/642] phrase of another antifascist—a matter of taste. He can, in Mr. Rahv's sense of the word, *experience* all the badness, but he cannot deal with it, he dare not judge it.

In the end it kills him. And Hemingway knows, of course, that it kills him and is at pains to make it clear that, of all the things that prevent Robert Jordan's dispatch from arriving in time to halt the ill-fated attack, it is the atmosphere of Gaylord's Hotel that is ultimately culpable; it is Marty's protected madness that seals Jordan's fate. Were this kept in focus we should have had a personal tragedy which would have truly represented the whole tragedy of the Spanish war—the tragedy, that is, which was not merely a defeat by a superior force but also a moral and political failure; for tragedy is not a matter of fact, it is a matter of value. To Robert Jordan his own death is bitter enough, but only as the ultimate incident of his experience. Of its inherent meaning, of its significance in relation to its cause, he has no awareness. Nor is his lack of awareness an intentional irony of which the reader is to be conscious. Hemingway lets the casual [*sic*] significance fade, and Jordan's death becomes very nearly a matter of accident. The book seems to wish to say that the loving and brave will be separated and killed unless men realize their unending community; but it is not only a lack of community that kills Robert Jordan, it is all that is implied by Gaylord's Hotel and André Marty.

It is almost terrifying to see where an author can be led in unintentional falsification by his devotion to naked "experience." Hemingway knows that his hero must die in *some* moral circumstance; he lamely and belatedly contrives for Robert Jordan a problem of—courage. And so we get what we all like, and rightly like, a good fighting death, but in the face of all that Jordan's death truly signifies, this is devastatingly meaningless. Courage, we are told in a last word, is all: and every nerve responds to the farewell, the flying hoofs, the pain and the pathos, but we have been shuffled quite away from tragedy, which is not of the nerves but of judgment and the mind.

The major movement of the novel is, then, a failure, and a failure the more to be regretted because it has so many of the elements of great success. There is another movement of the novel that cannot be judged by quite the same standards of political intelligence—I mean all that part which deals with the guerrilla bands of the mountains. To judge this, one has to understand its genre; one has to see this part of the story as a social romance. I should like to draw on Mr. Rahv again: he remarks in another of his essays ("Pale-face and Redskin," *Kenyon Review*, Summer, 1939) that Hemingway may well be under- [642/643] stood as a descendant of Natty Bumppo. Certainly in each of Hemingway's heroes there is a great deal of the

Leatherstocking blood, though "crossed" (as Leatherstocking himself would say) with the gentler, more sensitive blood of Uncas. And as Leatherstocking-Uncas, the perfect scout, Robert Jordan is all decision, action, and good perception, far more interesting and attractive than in his character of looker-on at the political feats of the Russians where he is a kind of Parsifal, the culpable innocent who will not ask the right questions. But more than the character of this hero takes its rise from Cooper—more, too, than Hemingway's "sense of terrain" which Edmund Wilson speaks of as being like Cooper's. For when we think of how clear a line there is between Uncas, Chingachgook and Tamenund, the noble Indians, and El Sordo and Anselmo and the rest of the guerrilla band, we see how very like Cooper's is Hemingway's romantic sense of the social and personal virtues.

With Cooper, however, the social idealization is more formal, more frankly "mythical"—he does not quite require that we really believe in his Indians, only learn from them. But Hemingway does want us to believe in his guerrillas with their strange, virtuous Indian-talk, and he wants us to love them. We cannot truly believe in them. And we cannot quite love them because we sense, as we usually do in a love affair between a writer and a virtuous nation or people or class—such as between Kipling and the sahibs or, to speak of a minor but socially interesting writer of today, between Angela Thirkell and the English upper middle class—that there is pretty sure to appear, sooner or later, a hatred of the outlander. If one cannot make an identification with Hemingway's guerrillas—and it is difficult—they suggest their own unique and superior moral charm rather than the human community the novel undertakes to celebrate.

There is something pretty suspect, too, in the love-story of this novel, which has so stirred and charmed the reviewers. By now the relation between men and women in Hemingway's novels has fixed itself into a rather dull convention according to which the men are all dominance and knowledge, the women all essential innocence and responsive passion. These relationships reach their full development almost at the moment of the first meeting and are somehow completed as soon as begun. Most significant, one feels of love in the Hemingway novels that it can exist at all only because circumstances so surely doom it. We do not have to venture very deep into unexpressed meanings to find a connection between Hemingway's social myth and the pattern of his love stories—in both there is a desperation [**643/644**] which makes a quick grab for simple perfection. This desperation makes understandable the compulsive turning to courage as the saving and solving virtue. The whole complex of attitudes is, we might say, a way of responding to the imminent idea of death.

I am by no means in agreement with the many critics who, in writing about Hemingway, have expressed their annoyance that anyone should deal with death except as a simple physical fact. I am far from sure that our liberal, positive, progressive attitudes have taught us to be emotionally more competent before the idea of death, but only more silent; and I certainly do not assume that anyone is committing a political misdemeanor when he breaks our habit of silence. Yet in Hemingway's response to the idea of death there is something indirect and thwarted, as though he had not wholly escaped our reticences to meditate freely upon the theme, as could, say, a death-haunted man like John Donne, from whom Hemingway takes the epigraph and title of his novel. For Donne, death is the appalling negation and therefore the teacher of the ego. For Hemingway, death is the ego's final expression and the perfect protector of the personality. It is a sentimental error from which Donne was saved by his great power of mind. And it was from Donne's truer response to death that he learned the true nature of the ego, how little it can exist by itself, how "no man is an *Ilande* intire of itselfe." Hemingway, so much at the service of the cult of experience, debars himself from what Donne learned from his contemplation of death. As a consequence, it is the isolation of the individual ego in its search for experience that Hemingway celebrates in this novel that announces as its theme the community of men.

PHILIP YOUNG

Loser Take Nothing

A Farewell to Arms (1929) which borrows its title from a poem of that name by George Peele,[1] reverts to the war and supplies background for *The Sun Also Rises*. For the germs of both of its plots, a war plot and a love plot, it reaches back to *In Our Time*. An outline of the human arms in the novel is to be found among these early stories in a piece called "A Very Short Story." This sketch, less than two pages long, dealt quickly, as the novel does extensively, with the drinking and love-making in an Italian hospital of an American soldier, wounded in the leg, and a nurse, and had told of their love and their wish to get married. But where the book ends powerfully with the death in childbirth of the woman, the story dribbled off in irony. The lovers parted, the soldier leaving for home to get a job so that he could send for his sweetheart. Before long, however, the nurse wrote that she had a new lover who was going to marry her, though he never did; and then, shortly after receiving the letter, the soldier "contracted gonorrhea from a sales girl in a loop department store while riding in a taxicab through Lincoln Park."[2]

The war plot of *A Farewell to Arms*, on the other hand, is a greatly expanded version of that Chapter VI sketch in which Nick was wounded and made his separate peace—with Rinaldi, who also appears in the longer work. This wound, which got Nick in the spine, and "I" in the knee, and emasculated Jake, has returned to the knee, which is where Hemingway was most badly hit. Then the same story is rehearsed again in lengthened form.

[From Ernest Hemingway: A Reconsideration © 1966 by Philip Young]

Recuperated enough to return to action after another convalescence in Milan, Lt. Frederic Henry becomes bitter about the society responsible for the war and, caught up in the Italian retreat from Caporetto, he breaks utterly with the army in which he is an officer. And this is again the old protagonist, who cannot sleep at night for thinking—who must not use his head to think with, and will absolutely have to stop it. He is also the man who, when he does sleep, has nightmares, and wakes from them in sweat and fright, and goes back to sleep in an effort to stay outside his dreams.

Unlike Jake Barnes, however, Frederic Henry participates fully in the book's action, and as a person is wholly real. But he is also a little more than that, for just as the response of Americans of the period to the aimless and disillusioned hedonism of Jake and his friends indicated that some subtle chord in them had been struck, so something in the evolution of Frederic Henry from complicity in the war to bitterness and escape has made him seem, though always himself, a little larger that that, too. Complicity, bitterness, escape—a whole country could read its experience, Wilson to Harding, in his, and it began to become clear that in Hemingway as elsewhere "hero" meant not simply "protagonist" but a man who stands for many men. Thus it is that when historians of various kinds epitomize the temper of the American Twenties and a reason for it the adventures of that lieutenant come almost invariably to mind. And also, since these things could hardly be said better, his words:

> I was always embarrassed by the words sacred, glorious, and sacrifice and the expression in vain. We had heard them, sometimes standing in the rain almost out of earshot, so that only the shouted words came through... now for a long time, and I had seen nothing sacred, and the things that were glorious had no glory and the sacrifices were like the stock yards at Chicago if nothing was done with the meat except to bury it.... Abstract words such as glory, honor, courage, or hallow were obscene....

It is on the implications of these sentiments, and in order to escape a certain death which he has not deserved, that Henry finally acts. He jumps in a river and deserts: the hell with it. It was an unforgettable plunge.

Memorable too, in her devotion and her ordeal—though much less memorable, and much less real—is Henry's English mistress. Idealized past the fondest belief of most people, and even the more realistic wishes of some, compliant, and bearing unmistakable indications of the troubles to come when she will appear as mistress of heroes to come, Catherine Barkley has at least some character in her own right, and is both the first true "Hemingway heroine," and the most convincing one. Completely real, once again and at once, are the minor characters—especially Rinaldi, the ebullient Italian doctor, and the priest, and Count Greffi, the ancient billiard player, and the enlisted ambulance drivers.

Chiefly, again, it is their speech which brings these people to life and keeps them living. The rest of the book, however, is less conversational in tone than before, and in other ways the writing is changed a little. The sentences are now longer, even lyrical, on occasion, and, once in a while, experimental, as Hemingway, not content to rest in the style that had made him already famous, tries for new effects, and does not always succeed. Taken as a whole, however, his prose has never been finer or more finished than in this novel. Never have those awesome, noncommittal understatements, which say more than could ever be written out, been more impressive. The book has passages which rate with the hardest, cleanest and most moving in contemporary literature.

The novel has one stylistic innovation that is important to it. This is the use of an object, rain, in a way that cannot be called symbolic so much as portentous. Hemingway had used water as a metaphoric purge of past experience before, and so Henry's emergence from the river into a new life, as from a total immersion, was not new. What is new in *A Farewell to Arms* is the consistent use of rain as a signal of disaster. Henry, in his practical realism, professes a disbelief in signs, and tells himself that Catherine's vision of herself dead in the rain is meaningless. But she dies in it and actually, glancing back at the end, one sees that a short, introductory scene at the very start of the book had presented an ominous conjunction of images—rain, pregnancy and death—which set the mood for all that was to follow, prefigured it and bound all the ends of the novel into a perfect and permanent knot.

This is really the old "pathetic fallacy" put to new use, and—since there is no need to take it scientifically or philosophically, but simply as a subtle and unobtrusive device for unity—quite an acceptable one, too. Good and bad weather go along with good and bad moods and events. It is not just that, like everyone, the characters respond emotionally to conditions of atmosphere, light and so on, but that there is a correspondence between these things and their fate. They win when it's sunny, and lose in the rain.

Thus, then, the weather, which as both omen and descriptive background (made once again to count for something) is a matter of style, cannot be extricated from the book's plot, or structure. This is of course built on the two themes involved in the ambiguity of "arms," which are developed and intensified together, with alternating emphasis, until at the extremity of one the hero escapes society, and the heroine everything. Despite the frequency with which they appear in the same books, the themes of love and war are really an unlikely pair, if not indeed—to judge from the frequency with which writers fail to wed them—quite incompatible. But in Hemingway's novel their courses run straight and exactly, though subtly, parallel, and he has managed to fuse them. In his affair with the war Henry goes from desultory participation to serious action and a wound, and then through his recuperation in Milan to a retreat which leads to his desertion. His relationship with Catherine Barkley undergoes six precisely corresponding stages—from a trifling sexual affair to actual love and her conception, and then through her confinement in the Alps to a trip to the hospital which leads to her death. By the end of Hemingway's novel, when the last farewell is taken, the two stories are as one, in the point that is made very clear, lest there be any sentimental doubt about it, that life, both social and personal, is a struggle in which the Loser Takes Nothing, either.

This ideology, which is the novel's, has two related aspects which are implicit in the united elements of the plot. In the end, a man is trapped. He is trapped biologically—in this case by the "natural" process that costs him his future wife in the harrowing scenes at the hospital, and is trapped by society—at the end of a retreat, where you take off or get shot. Either way it can only end badly, and there are no other ways. How you will get it, though, depends on the kind of person you are:

> If people bring so much courage to this world the world has to kill them to break them, so of course it kills them. The world breaks everyone and afterward many are strong at the broken places. But those that will not break it kills. It kills the very good and the very gentle and the very brave impartially. If you are none of these you can be sure that it will kill you too but there will be no special hurry.

It does not really matter very much that there is something a little romantic about this passage, perhaps the finest in all of Hemingway, or that the novel is a romantic one as a whole. It must be just about the most romantic piece of realistic fiction, or the most realistic romance, in our literature. Henry's love affair, which blossoms glamorously from the mud of the war, is but the most striking of several factors which go together to make his war a remarkably pleasant one, as wars go, and much more attractive than wars actually are. The lieutenant has a somewhat special time of it, with orderlies and porters and little or no trouble with superiors, and good wine and good food and a lot of free time in which to enjoy them. But it is not important that these aspects of his army experience are highly untypical. Nor does it matter on the other hand that women usually survive childbirth, and many men are discharged from armies in good shape, and then life goes on much as before. What matters instead is that this time Hemingway has made his story, and the attitudes it enacts, persuasive and compelling within the covers of his book. And after we have closed the covers there is no inclination to complain that this was, after all, no literal transcription of reality which exaggerated neither the bitter nor the sweet. It was rather an intensification of life. Willingly or not, disbelief is suspended before a vision that overrides objections, withers preconceptions and even memory and imposes itself in their place.

This novel has the last word, always. Catherine Barkley, as it happened, was very good, very gentle, very brave. Unlike the hero, who broke and survived to become eventually quite strong, she would not break and so she was killed. It was very likely in rebuttal to the people who rejected the pessimism of this denouement that Hemingway pointed out three years later, in *Death in the Afternoon*, that love stories do not end happily in life, either:

> There is no lonelier man in death, except the suicide, than that manwho has lived many years with a good wife and then outlived her. If two people love each other there can be no happy end to it.

Chronology

1899	Born Ernest Miller Hemingway on July 21 in Oak Park, Illinois
1917	Graduates from Oak Park High School; works as a reporter for the *Kansas City Star*.
1918	Enlists in Red Cross Ambulance Corps; wounded in Italy on July 8
1920	Begins writing for the *Toronto Star* newspapers
1921	Marries Elizabeth Hadley Richardson; moves to Paris, France
1923	Attends first bullfight in Spain; publishes *Three Stories and Ten Poems*; moves to Toronto; son John (Bumby) is born
1924	Returns to Paris; publishes *in our time* in Europe
1925	Publishes *In Our Time* in America
1926	Publishes *The Torrents of Spring* and *The Sun Also Rises*
1927	Divorces Hadley Richardson; marries Pauline Pfeiffer; publishes *Men Without Women*
1928	Moves to Key West, Florida; son Patrick is born
1929	Publishes *A Farewell to Arms*
1931	Son Gregory is born
1932	Publishes *Death in the Afternoon*
1933	Publishes *Winner Take Nothing*; begins first African safari

1935   Publishes *Green Hills of Africa*

1937   Begins covering Spanish Civil War for the North American Newspaper Alliance; publishes *To Have and Have Not*

1938   Publishes *The Fifth Column and the First Forty-nine Stories*

1940   Publishes *For Whom the Bell Tolls*; divorces Pauline Pfeiffer; marries Martha Gellhorn; buys Finca Vigia estate in Cuba

1944   Serves as war correspondent in Europe; suffers concussion in serious auto accident

1945   Divorces Martha Gellhorn

1946   Marries Mary Welsh

1950   Publishes *Across the River and into the Trees*

1952   Publishes *The Old Man and the Sea*

1953   Awarded Pulitzer Prize for fiction for 1952; begins second African safari

1954   Suffers major injuries in two plane crashes in Africa; receives Nobel Prize in literature

1961   Commits suicide in Ketchum, Idaho, on July 2

1964   *A Moveable Feast* is published

1970   *Islands in the Stream* is published

1985   *The Dangerous Summer* is published

1986   *The Garden of Eden* is published

1999   *True at First Light* is published

Works by Ernest Hemingway

Three Stories and Ten Poems. 1923.

in our time. 1924.

In Our Time: Stories. 1925.

The Torrents of Spring. 1926.

Today Is Friday. (pamphlet) 1926.

The Sun Also Rises. 1926.

Men Without Women. 1927.

A Farewell to Arms. 1929.

Death in the Afternoon. 1932.

God Rest You Merry Gentlemen. (pamphlet) 1933.

Winner Take Nothing. 1933.

Green Hills of Africa. 1935.

To Have and Have Not. 1937.

The Spanish Earth. (film transcript) 1938.

The Fifth Column and the First Forty-nine Stories. 1938.

For Whom the Bell Tolls. 1940.

Men at War: The Best War Stories of All Time (editor). 1942.

Voyage to Victory: An Eye-witness Report of the Battle for a Normandy Beachhead. 1944.

The Portable Hemingway. Ed. Malcolm Cowley. 1944

Selected Short Stories. c. 1945.

The Essential Hemingway. 1947.

Across the River and into the Trees. 1950.

The Old Man and the Sea. 1952.

The Hemingway Reader. Ed. Charles Poore. 1953.

Two Christmas Tales. 1959.

Collected Poems. 1960.

The Snows of Kilimanjaro and Other Stories. 1961.

The Wild Years. Ed. Gene Z. Hanrahan. 1962.

A Moveable Feast. 1964.

By-Line: Ernest Hemingway: Selected Articles and Dispatches of Four Decades. Ed. William White. 1967.

The Fifth Column and Four Stories of the Spanish Civil War. 1969.

Ernest Hemingway, Cub Reporter. Ed. Matthew J. Bruccoli. 1970.

Islands in the Stream. 1970.

Ernest Hemingway's Apprenticeship: Oak Park 1916-1917. Ed. Matthew J. Bruccoli. 1971.

The Nick Adams Stories. 1972.

88 Poems. Ed. Nicholas Gerogiannis. 1979, 1992 (as *Complete Poems*).

Selected Letters 1917-1961. Ed. Carlos Baker. 1981.

The Dangerous Summer. 1985.

Dateline, Toronto: Hemingway's Complete Toronto Star *Dispatches, 1920-1924.* Ed. William White. 1985.

The Garden of Eden. 1986.

Complete Short Stories. 1987.

Remembering Spain: Hemingway's Civil War Eulogy and the Veterans of the Abraham Lincoln Brigade. Ed. Cary Nelson. 1994.

True at First Light, 1999.

Works about Ernest Hemingway

Asselineau, Roger, ed. *The Literary Reputation of Hemingway in Europe*. NY: New York University Press, 1965.

Baker, Carlos. *Ernest Hemingway: A Life Story*. NY: Charles Scribner's Sons, 1969.

———. *Hemingway: The Writer as Artist*. Princeton, NJ: Princeton University Press, 1952.

Benson, Jackson, J, ed. *The Short Stories of Ernest Hemingway: Critical Essays*. Durham: Duke University Press, 1975.

Bloom Harold, ed. *Ernest Hemingway's The Old Man and The Sea*. Philadelphia: Chelsea House, 1999.

———. *Bloom's Major Short Story Writers: Ernest Hemingway*. Philadelphia, PA: Chelsea House, 1999.

———. *Ernest Hemingway*. New York: Chelsea House Publishers, 1985.

———. *Modern Critical Interpretations: A Farewell to Arms*. New York: Chelsea House, 1987.

Brian, Denis. *The True Gen: An Intimate Portrait of Ernest Hemingway By Those Who Knew Him*. NY: Grove Press, 1988.

Brooks, Cleanth. *The Hidden God: Studies in Hemingway, Faulkner, Yeats, Eliot, and Warren*. New Haven: Yale University Press, 1963.

Bruccoli, Matthew J. ed. *The Only Thing That Counts: The Ernest Hemingway-Maxwell Perkins Correspondence*. Columbia: University of South Carolina

Burgess, Anthony. *Ernest Hemingway and His World*. NY: Charles Scribner's Sons, 1978.

Diliberto, Gioia. *Hadley*. NY: Ticknor & Fields, 1992.

Donaldson, Scott. *By Force of Will: the Life and Art of Ernest Hemingway*. NY: The Viking Press, 1977.

———. *The Cambridge Companion to Hemingway*. Cambridge: Cambridge University Press, 1999.

Eby, Carl P. *Hemingway's Fetishism: Psychoanalysis and the Mirror of Manhood*. Albany: State University of New York Press, 1999.

Gellens, Jay. Ed. *A Farewell to Arms: A Collection of Critical Essays*. Englewood Cliffs, NJ: Prentice-Hall, 1970.

Gurko, Leo. *Ernest Hemingway and the Pursuit of Heroism*. NY: Thomas Y. Crowell Co., 1968.

Hemingway, Gregory H. *Papa: A Personal Memoir*. Boston: Houghton Mifflin, 1976.

Hemingway, Leicester. *My Brother, Ernest Hemingway*. Cleveland: World Publishing Company, 1962.

Hemingway, Mary Walsh. *How It Was*. NY: Alfred A. Knopf, 1976.

Hotchner, A. E. *Papa Hemingway: A Personal Memoir*. NY: Carroll & Graf Publishers, Inc., 1955.

Kert, Bernice. *The Hemingway Women*. New York: W.W. Norton & Company, 1983.

Lynn, Kenneth S. *Hemingway*. New York: Simon and Schuster, 1987.

McDaniel, Melissa. *Ernest Hemingway: Writer*. Philadelphia: Chelsea House, 1997.

McLendon, James. *Papa Hemingway in Key West*. Miami, Florida: E.A. Seemann Publishing, Inc., 1972.

Mellow, James R. *Hemingway: A Life Without Consequences*. Boston: Houghton Mifflin Company, 1992.

Pavloska, Susanna.*Modern Primitives: Race and Language in Gertrude Stein, Ernest Hemingway, and Zora Neale Hurston*. New York: Garland Publishing, 2000.

Reynolds, Michael. *Hemingway: The Final Years*. New York: W.W. Norton & Company, 2000.

———. *Hemingway: The Paris Years*. Oxford, UK: Basil Blackwell, Ltd., 1989.

Sanford, Marcelline Hemingway. *At the Hemingways: A Family Portrait*. Boston: Little, Brown and Company, 1961.

Szumski, Bonnie, ed. *Readings on The Old Man and the Sea*. San Diego: Greenhaven Press, 1999.

Villard, Henry Serrano and James Nagel. *Hemingway In Love and War: The Lost Diary of Agnes von Kurowsky, Her Letters, and Correspondence of Ernest Hemingway*. Boston: Northeastern University Press, 1989.

Weeks, Robert, P, ed. *Hemingway: A Collection of Critical Essays*. Englewood Cliffs, NJ: Prentice-Hall, 1962.

Young, Philip. *Ernest Hemingway: A Reconsideration*. Pennsylvania State University Press, 1966.

Contributors

HAROLD BLOOM is Sterling Professor of the Humanities at Yale University and Henry W. and Albert A. Berg Professor of English at the New York University Graduate School. He is the author of over 20 books, including *Shelly's Mythmaking* (1959), *The Visionary Company* (1961), *Blake's Apocalypse* (1963), *Yeats* (1970), *A Map of Misreading* (1975), *Kabbalah and Criticism* (1975), *Agon: Toward a Theory of Revisionism* (1982), *The American Religion* (1992), *The Western Canon* (1994), and *Omens of Millennium: The Gnosis of Angels, Dreams, and Resurrection* (1996). *The Anxiety of Influence* (1973) sets forth Professor Bloom's provocative theory of the literary relationships between the great writers and their predecessors. His most recent books include *Shakespeare: The Invention of the Human*, a 1998 National Book Award finalist, and *How to Read and Why*, which was published in 2000. In 1999, Professor Bloom received the prestigious American Academy of Arts and Letters Gold Medal for Criticism.

VEDA BOYD JONES is the author of over twenty children's books and has had articles published in *The Writer*, *Writer's Digest*, and *Woman's World*. Jones earned an MA in history at the University of Arkansas and currently teaches for the Institute of Children's Literature.

ISOBEL O'DONNELL writes poetry, fiction and essays in criticism. She attended Rosemont College where she was a recipient of the Margaret G. Humphrey Award for Creative Writing, as well as the *Thorn* Poetry Award, and is a two-time winner of the Essay Award.

EDMUND WILSON (1895-1972) was a major literary critic in his time. His works include *The Wound and the Bow*, *The Shores of Light*, *The Patriotic Gore* and *Axel's Castle*, a study of symbolism. He also wrote a novel, short stories, and plays. He served on the staffs of the *New Republic* from 1926-1931 and the *New Yorker* from 1944-1948.

LIONEL TRILLING (1905-1975) wrote on numerous literary topics, and was a respected critic during his career. His selected essays in criticism have been collected in *The Liberal Imagination*, *The Opposing Self*, and *A Gathering of Fugitives*. Other works include critical studies of Matthew Arnold and E. M. Forster. He was Professor of English at Columbia University from 1932.

PHILIP YOUNG was professor of American Literature at Pennsylvania State University from 1959-1966. He has also served as a research professor of English Literature and a Fulbright lecturer in France and Italy. His writings on Hemingway include: *Ernest Hemingway: A Reconsideration*; *By-Line Ernest Hemingway*; *The Hemingway Manuscripts: An Inventory*, with Charles W. Mann; and *The Nick Adams Stories*.

Notes

NOTES FROM HEMINGWAY'S SECRET CODES

1 Samuel Taylor Coleridge, "The Rime of the Ancient Mariner," from "The Argument," 1798. *The Norton Anthology of English Literature,* Fifth Edition, M.H. Abrams, ed. (New York: Norton, 1986).

2 Coleridge, "The Rime of the Ancient Mariner," line 615.

3 Coleridge, "The Rime of the Ancient Mariner," epigraph. In the Latin epigraph to Coleridge's work, he adapts Thomas Burnet's *Archeologiae philosophicae* (1692), "*Facile credo, plures esse Naturas invisibiles quam visibiles in rerum universitate...Harum rerum notitiam semper ambivit ingenium humanum, nunquam attigit...Sed veritati interea invigilandum est, modusque servandus, ut certa ab incertis, diem a nocte, distinguamus.*"

4 Ben Stoltzfus, "Hemingway, Malraux and Spain: *For Whom the Bell Tolls* and *L'espoir,*" Comparative Literature Studies 36.3 (1999) 181, 23 March 2001 <http://muse.jhu.edu/journals/comparative_literature_studies/v036/36.3stoltzfus .html

5 A. Scott Berg, ed., *Max Perkins, Editor of Genius.* (New York: Riverhead, Berkley Publishing Group, 1978) 95-97.

6 Matthew J. Bruccoli, ed. *The Only Thing That Counts: The Ernest Hemingway-Maxwell Perkins Correspondence.* (Columbia: University of South Carolina, 1996)Bruccoli, 44.

7 Berg, 100.

8 Matthew J. Bruccoli *The Only Thing That Counts: The Ernest Hemingway-Maxwell Perkins Correspondence.* (Columbia: University of South Carolina, 1996) 40.

9 Philip Young, "Loser Takes Nothing," *A Farewell to Arms: A Collection of Critical Essays,* ed. Jay Gellens (Englewood Cliffs, NJ: Prentice-Hall, 1970) 29.

10 Carlos Baker, "The Spanish Tragedy," *Ernest Hemingway: Critiques of Four Major Novels.* (New York: Scribner's, 1962.) 123-128.

11 Baker, *Critiques of Four Major Novels* 123-128.

12 Lionel Trilling "An American in Spain," *Critiques of Four Major Novels.* Carlos Baker, ed.

NOTES FROM LOSER TAKE NOTHING

1 As in the case of many of Hemingway's titles, the allusion to the poem is slightly ironic, for Peele mourned the fact that he could no longer fight.

2 Except for the venereal element (which according to a paperback biographer was thus contracted by a *friend* of the author), it appears that this sketch tells how it actually was, the novel-to-be how it might have been. In life Catherine Barkley, the heroine of the novel, was Agnes H. von Kurowski, the Bellevue-trained daughter of a German-American father; Hemingway intended to bring her home from Italy and marry her. (Leicester's biography prints an excellent photograph of her; Marcelline's biography prints a picture Ernest sent home from Italy of a "nice-looking bearded older man... Count Greppie"—possibly the model for Count Greffi in the novel.)

Index